Library Skills Activities Kit
Puzzles, Games, Bulletin Boards, and Other Interest-Rousers for the Elementary School Library

Jerry J. Mallett, Ed.D.

Professor of Education
Findlay College
Findlay, Ohio

Jerry J. Mallett, Ed.D., has been actively involved in elementary education for more than 15 years as a classroom teacher, reading specialist, school principal, and professor. Awarded his doctorate by the University of Toledo in 1972, he is presently Professor of Education at Findlay College, Findlay, Ohio.

Dr. Mallett is the author of many articles on reading instruction and editor of *The Reading Clinic,* a monthly publishing program which provides practical new ideas, techniques, and materials for reading instruction. He is also the author of the *Classroom Reading Games Activities Kit* (1975) and *101 Make-and-Play Reading Games for the Intermediate Grades* (1976), both published by The Center.

The Center for Applied Research in Education, Inc.
West Nyack, New York 10994

© 1981 by

THE CENTER FOR APPLIED
RESEARCH IN EDUCATION, INC.

West Nyack, New York

All rights reserved.

Permission is given for individual librarians, classroom teachers, and reading specialists to reproduce the student puzzle sheets and illustrations for library or classroom use. Reproduction of these materials for an entire school system is strictly forbidden.

**For my parents, to whom I owe much,
George and Myrtle Mallett**

Library of Congress Cataloging in Publication Data

Mallett, Jerry J.
    Library skills activities kit.

    Includes index.
    1. School children—Library orientation.
2. School libraries. I. Title.
Z718.1.M27   025.5'678   81-1290
ISBN 0-87628-535-3   AACR2

Printed in the United States of America

About this Sourcebook of Library Activities

The *Library Skills Activities Kit* has two primary purposes: to help you expand children's interest in reading and in the library media center and to help you teach functional library skills. For easy use in selecting activities, it is organized into the following five sections:

      I. LIBRARY INTEREST ROUSERS
     II. BULLETIN BOARDS
    III. BULLETIN BOARD ACTIVITIES
    IV. PUZZLE PAGES
     V. LIBRARY SKILLS GAMES

In addition, the *Kit* provides a convenient Skills Index for quick location of activities in each section appropriate to the teaching and reinforcing of particular library skills.

Included are more than 20 creative ideas to stimulate children to want to read... 16 unique bulletin board displays to promote reading of library books... 15 learning bulletin board activities to reinforce library skills... 47 enjoyable puzzle activities to give children practice in specific skills ... and 29 individual and small group games to teach and reinforce a variety of skills. And each of these ideas, bulletin boards, and activities is complete, keyed to recommended grade levels for use, and ready for your immediate use in your own library media center.

As a further aid to you, all materials are printed in a large 8½" × 11" comb-bound format that folds back flat for easy use and copying. Moreover, the puzzle sheets can be duplicated just as they appear and as many times as you need for individual or group use. They also include complete answer keys for quick checking of children's work by you or by the children themselves. In addition, there are scores of full-size patterns you can copy in making games, bulletin boards, and special interest-rousers.

You will find that the *Library Skills Activities Kit*:

- helps you motivate children to read a variety of books.
- helps you involve children actively in the library media center.
- offers a practical, simple, yet stimulating way to give children the necessary drill on library skills.
- provides interesting and productive activities for both individuals and groups of children.

About this Sourcebook of Library Activities

- utilizes simple, commonplace materials normally found in most libraries.
- is especially helpful in sparking initiative in reluctant readers.
- includes activities to help children learn more than a dozen specific library skills, among them: guide word usage, location of fiction books, card catalog usage, alphabetization, Dewey decimal classification, and use of the encyclopedia.

It is hoped that this sourcebook will provide a continuing, year-round source of practical, ready-to-use ideas and activities to enrich, revitalize, and reinforce all aspects of your library program.

Jerry J. Mallett

Table of Contents

About This Sourcebook of Library Activities iii

I. Library Interest-Rousers 1

    Rub-a-Dub Reading Tub • 3
    Month of the Monsters • 3
        Monster Mania Activity Sheet — 4
        Monster Bulletin Board — 5
        Monster Mobile — 6
        Monster Button — 6
        Monster Reading Center — 7
        Monster Game — 8
    Book Mobiles • 10
    Bookmarks • 15
    Book Lists for Children • 18
        A Barrel of the WINNERS! — 19
        A Grab Bag of Super Books About Families — 21
        A Galaxy of Good Books About Holidays — 23
        Books That Make You Giggle and Grin! — 25
        Books That Weave a Magic Spell of Fantasy! — 27
        A Basket of Beautiful Informational Books — 29
        Books to Make You Shudder — 31
        Pass the Poetry Please! — 33
        A Pocket Filled with Books About Our Past — 35
        Who Done It Books — 37
    Basket of the Best • 39
    Book Jacket Puzzles • 39
    A Peach of a Good Book • 40
    Write to Your Favorite Author • 41
    Bee in the Know • 42
    Hang Up Your Reading • 44
    Stop ... Look ... Listen! • 44
    Be a Book Promoter! • 45
    Book Factory • 46
    Local Author's Corner • 47
    Book Bazaar • 47
    Terrific Tweety Award • 47
    Marvelous Mysteries • 55

Library Interest-Rousers (cont'd)

Super Reader Award • 57
This Is a Recording • 59

II. Bulletin Boards 61

Put on Your Thinking Cap! • 63
Food for Thought • 66
Books We Went Buggy Over! • 68
Blooming Books • 72
If I Were ... • 74
Kick Up Your Heels ... and Write a Letter to an Author! • 77
Booootiful Books • 79
Be an Artist! • 83
Funniest Book I Ever Read • 85
Children's Book Week • 87
Unlock These Doors to Good Reading! • 89
Vote for Your Favorite "Little House" Book! • 91
Who Murdered Lady Quackle? • 94
Fabulous Fantasies! • 97
Nobel Prize for Literature • 100
Books About Our People! • 102

III. Bulletin Board Activities 105

Candy Factory • 107
Help Robbie Rabbit • 110
Feed the Elephants! • 113
Follow the Rainbow • 116
A Trip to Planet Gleet! • 119
It's Raining • 123
Robin's Roost • 126
Score! • 129
Sailing • 132
Surfing! • 135
See How High You Can Fly the Kite • 138
Can You Picture This? • 141
Quacker Questions • 143
A "Monsterous" Vocabulary • 146
Where's the Book? • 148

IV. Puzzle Pages 151

Shipshape • 155
A Table of What? • 157
Stairway to the Moon • 158

Contents

Puzzle Pages (cont'd)

Dave's Birthday • 159
The Balloon That Got Away! • 160
How Do You Know? • 161
Arrange the Books • 162
Take a Train Ride • 163
Which Drawer? • 164
Let's Take a Trip! • 165
Ski Jumping • 166
What Country Are We In? • 167
Follow the Rainbow • 168
My Favorite • 169
Oh No! • 170
Crossing Death Valley • 171
Symbols of America • 172
What a Score! • 173
An Artist • 174
Very Berry • 175
Be a Sport! • 176
Oh Gosh! • 177
Suppose You Knew ... • 178
Presidents Puzzle • 179
Dogs ... Dogs ... Dogs! • 180
Guide Word Puzzle • 181
Tree Mania! • 182
High-Rise Apartments! • 183
A Visit to Their Grandparents • 184
Buzz Off! • 185
The Surprise! • 186
Great Animals of the Past • 187
Index Information • 188
Look It Up! • 189
Deep in the Ocean • 190
Walk Through the Forest • 191
Colorful Contents • 192
The High Jump • 193
Help for Jack! • 194
It's Ancient History • 195
Who Let in the Dog? • 196
Follow the Flock! • 197
The Mystery at Skull Mountain • 198
In Chicago! • 199
Word Search Puzzle • 200
Did I Hear an S.O.S.? (cover page) • 201

Puzzle Pages (cont'd)
Super Sheets to the Rescue! (cover page) • 202
Answer Key to the Puzzle Sheets • 203

V. Library Skills Games **205**

Key Ring • 207
A Whale of a Good Time • 208
Traveling by Rail • 210
Apples, Oranges, and Lemons! • 212
Blast Off! • 215
Grand Prix • 216
Through the Night Sky • 218
Climb the Mountain • 220
Something's Fishy! • 222
Pick a Balloon • 224
Spin Out • 226
Table "Twirl" of Contents • 228
The Big "E" • 230
Rockets Away! • 232
Sad Sack • 235
Answer the Telephone • 237
Match to Win! • 239
Shelve 'Em! • 242
Who Shelved This? • 243
Hang It! • 245
Crazy Cards • 247
Find the Drawer • 250
Truckin' Down Highway 199 • 255
In This Book? • 262
Down Periscope • 266
Champ • 269
Cecil's Lotto Game • 271
Which Category? • 274

Skills Index **277**

I

Library Interest-Rousers

The activities in this section are designed to motivate children to want to read. The potpourri of ideas ranges from creative ways to display books to awards for both outstanding books *and* outstanding readers! Sample a few of these ideas and see if your book circulation doesn't begin to increase.

Title	Grade Level
Rub-a-Dub Reading Tub	primary
Month of the Monsters	primary-low intermediate
Book Mobiles	primary-intermediate
Bookmarks	primary-intermediate
Book Lists for Children	primary-intermediate
Basket of the Best	primary-intermediate
Book Jacket Puzzles	primary-intermediate
A Peach of a Good Book	primary-intermediate
Write to Your Favorite Author	primary intermediate
Bee in the Know	primary-intermediate
Hang Up Your Reading	primary-intermediate
Stop ... Look ... Listen!	primary-intermediate
Be a Book Promoter!	primary-intermediate
Book Factory	primary-intermediate
Local Author's Corner	primary-intermediate
Book Bazaar	primary-intermediate
Terrific Tweety Award	high primary-low intermediate
Marvelous Mysteries	high primary-intermediate
Super Reader Award	high primary-intermediate
This Is a Recording	intermediate

Library Interest-Rousers

RUB-A-DUB READING TUB

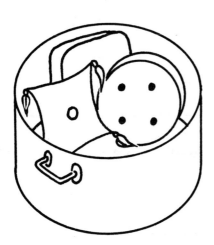

Find an appropriate corner for a large tub. Either paint the outer side of the tub or wrap it in bright Con-Tact paper. Throw in a few pillows and you have a ready-made "rub-a-dub reading tub!" Arrange a few picture books around it for "easy picking."

MONTH OF THE MONSTERS

Have a month of monsters! Here are several ideas to help you develop a monster-mania in your library.

Duplicate the "Monster-Mania" activity sheet, shown on the next page, and have copies available for children to complete after reading a "monster" book. Attach the completed sheets to the bulletin board display as shown on page 5.

Name _____

Date _____

MONSTER-MANIA

I just finished reading _____
_____

by _____

It (was—was not) very scary because _____
_____
_____
_____
_____

If I could change something in the story it would be _____
_____
_____
_____

The part I liked best was _____
_____
_____
_____
_____
_____
_____

Library Interest-Rousers

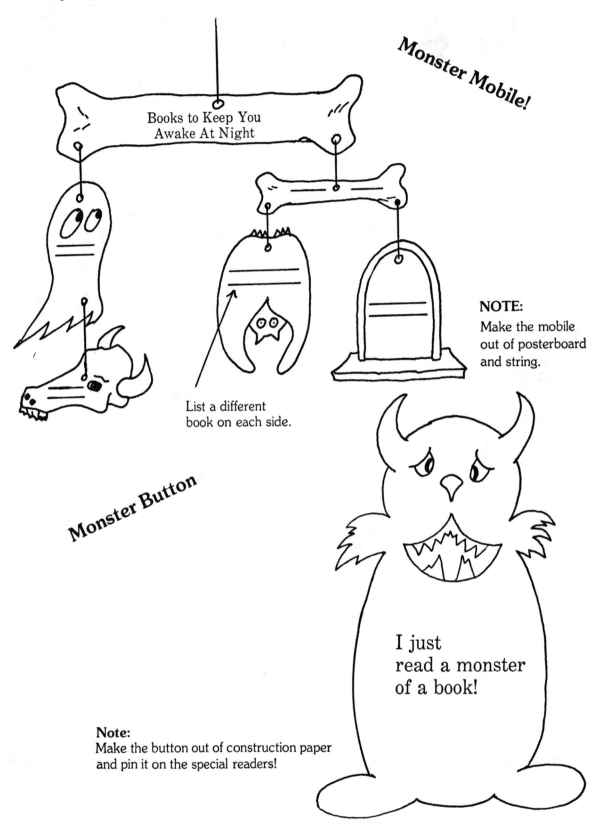

Library Interest-Rousers

Monster Reading Center!

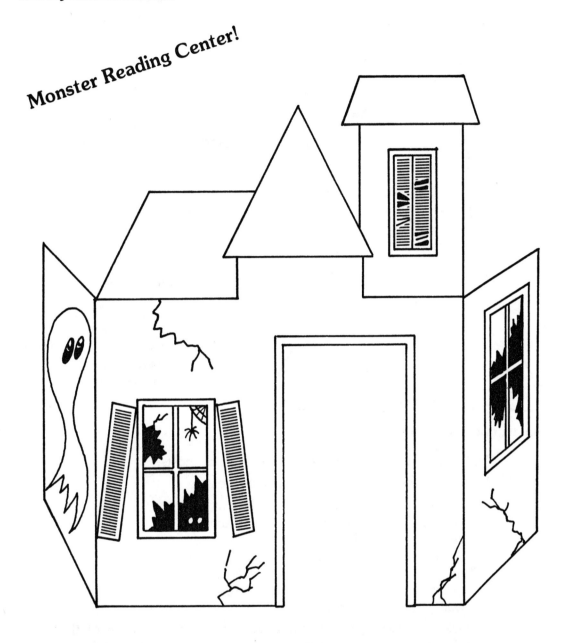

As shown in the illustration, a large cardboard box can be transformed easily into the front and sides of a haunted house. Simply use a razor-blade knife to cut out the door. Then add an eerie effect by illustrating the box with some latex paint. Fold back the sides of the box and use masking tape to attach the sides to the wall.

> **NOTE:** Be sure to draw or paint the window. Do not cut it out because this will weaken the structure of the box.

Library Interest-Rousers

Monster Game

Materials Needed:

4 pieces of 8" × 21" red posterboard
20 pieces of 3" × 4" white posterboard
felt-tipped pen
scissors

Construction Directions:

1. Cut the white posterboard pieces in the shape of ghosts.
2. Print one of the following words on each ghost.

bones	party	broom
cat	scream	costume
death	skeleton	frightened
goblin	Halloween	trick-or-treat
monster	witch	orange
prowl	shiver	terror
wail	zombie	

3. To make the four gameboards, trace nine ghosts on each of the red posterboard pieces, as shown in the illustration on the next page. Use one of the ghost cutouts as a pattern.
4. Print one of the following lists of words on the five ghosts on the left of each gameboard. Leave the ghosts on the right side of each gameboard blank.

List 1	List 2
black	dead
boo	fearful
candy	ghost
coffin	graveyard
dark	howl

Library Interest-Rousers

List 3	List 4
scared	jack-o'-lantern
shadow	night
shriek	parade
skull	pirate
tombstone	pumpkin

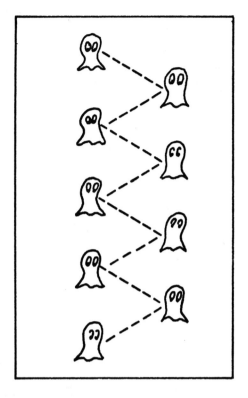

Have a Month of Monsters ......
... I insist!

Game Play:

1. Each player chooses a gameboard and places it in front of him/her.
2. All of the ghosts are dealt face down to the players. Players should not be able to see the words on each other's ghosts.
3. Players now look at the ghosts in their hands. If they have any words that can be placed in correct alphabetical order between two of the words on the gameboard, they should put these words on the appropriate blank ghosts.
4. The player who dealt the ghosts now begins the game by holding out the ghosts in his hand (word side down) to the player to his left. This player must take one of these ghosts. She must not show the word to any other player. If the word will fit in the correct alphabetical order on her gameboard, she places it on the appropriate blank ghost. If not, she simply adds it to the ghosts in her hand and continues the game by holding her ghosts (word side down) to the player to her left.
5. The game continues in this manner until one of the players fills in all of the blank ghosts on his or her gameboard. This player is the winner.

BOOK MOBILES

Make several of these mobiles and hang them in your library. Simply cut out different shapes and attach them with string as shown. By using an opaque projector you can easily trace the shapes on the posterboard. Now write appropriate book titles on both sides of the posterboard pieces.

> **NOTE:** You might ask several older students to make book mobiles of their own design to help decorate your library and create interest!

Library Interest-Rousers

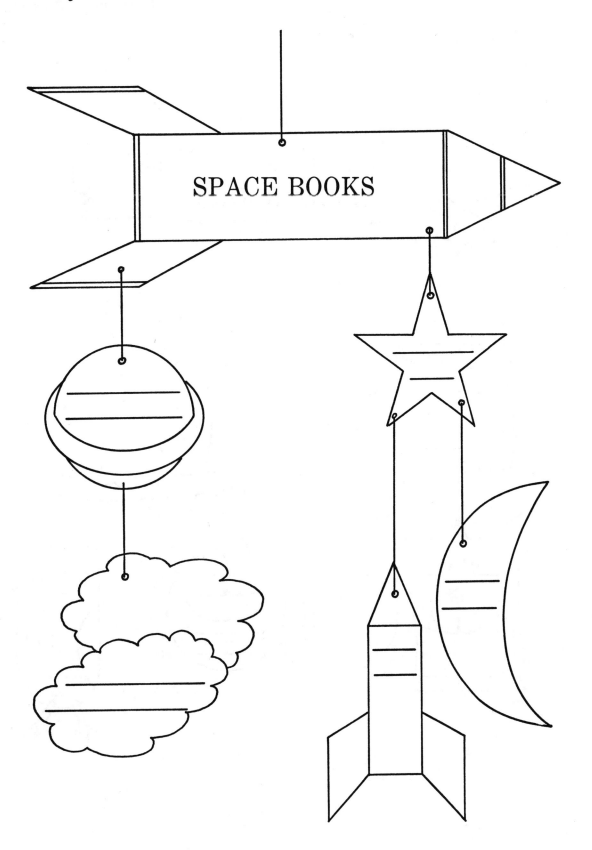

Library Interest-Rousers

Library Interest-Rousers

Library Interest-Rousers

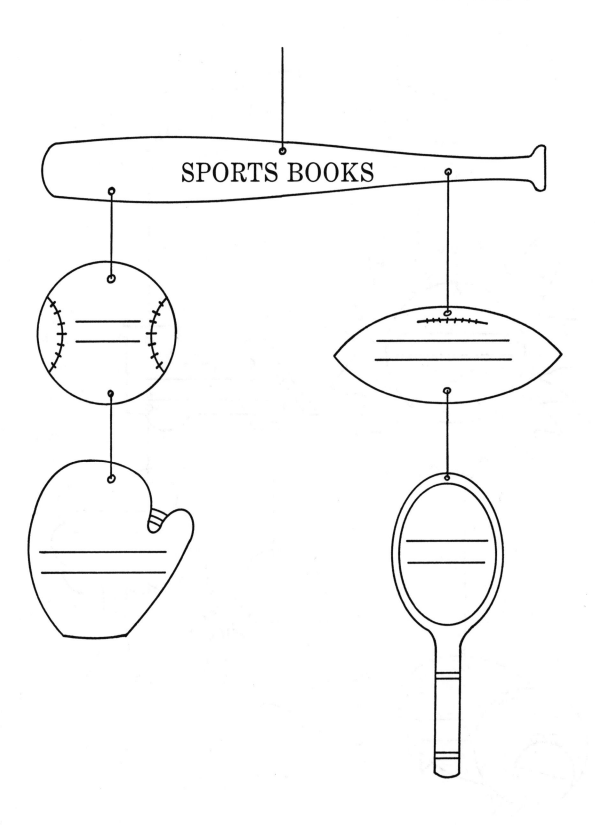

Library Interest-Rousers

BOOKMARKS

Children love to use special bookmarks for the books they are reading and they can make them out of construction paper.

> **NOTE:** You might want to put sample bookmarks on a poster and have the children make their own!

Some of the bookmarks shown on the next few pages are best saved for "special" readers! For example, the whale should go to one of your "regular customers."

15

Library Interest-Rousers

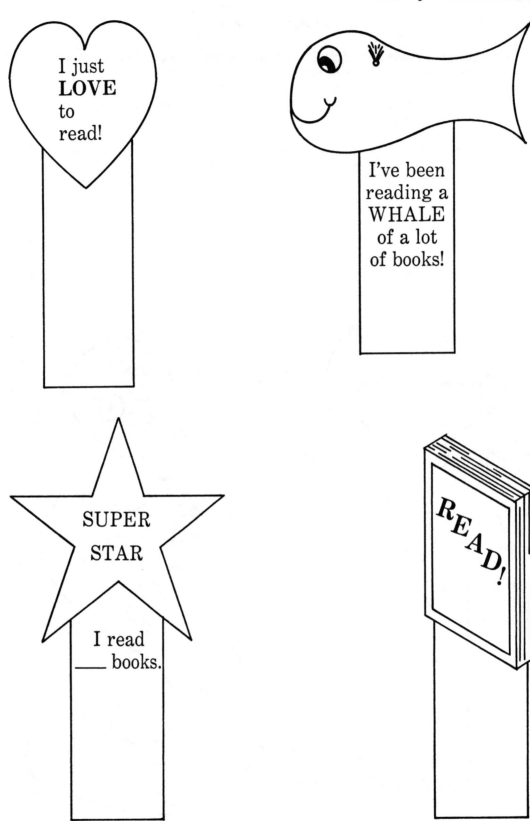

16

Library Interest-Rousers

Library Interest-Rousers

BOOK LISTS FOR CHILDREN

Promote reading by periodically offering clever book lists set in interesting formats. You may copy the ideas on the next pages along with a list of appropriate books. Place them in a very available location and just watch the books disappear!

Following each format are lists of books you might want to use with additions and deletions appropriate to your own collection.

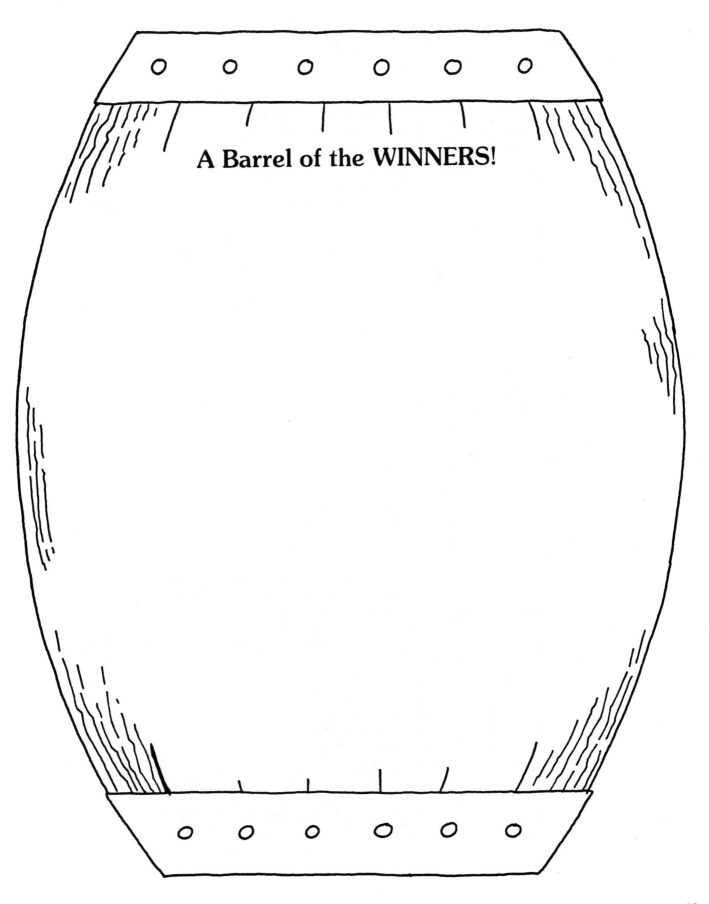

Library Interest-Rousers

Primary (Caldecott Medal Winners)

Bemelmans, Ludwig, *Madeline's Rescue,* Viking (1954)
Brown, Marcia, *Once a Mouse,* Scribner (1962)
Burton, Virginia Lee, *The Little House,* Houghton Mifflin (1943)
Emberley, Barbara, *Drummer Hoff,* Prentice-Hall (1968)
Hader, Berta and Elmer, *The Big Snow,* Macmillan (1949)
Handforth, Thomas, *Mei Li,* Doubleday (1939)
Hogrogian, Nonny, *One Fine Day,* Macmillan (1972)
Keats, Ezra Jack, *The Snowy Day,* Viking (1963)
Lipkind, William and Nicholas Mordvinoff, *Finders Keepers,* Harcourt, Brace Jovanovich (1952)
MacDonald, Golden, *The Little Island,* Doubleday (1947)
McCloskey, Robert, *Make Way for Ducklings,* Viking (1942)
McDermott, Gerald, *Arrow to the Sun,* Viking (1975)
Milhous, Katherine, *The Egg Tree,* Scribner (1951)
Ness, Evaline, *Sam, Bangs and Moonshine,* Holt, Rinehart & Winston (1967)
Politi, Leo, *Song of the Swallows,* Scribner (1950)
Sendak, Maurice, *Where the Wild Things Are,* Harper & Row (1964)
Steig, William, *Sylvester and the Magic Pebble,* Simon and Schuster (1970)
Tresselt, Alvin, *White Snow, Bright Snow,* Lothrop (1948)
Udry, Janice May, *A Tree Is Nice,* Harper & Row (1957)
Ward, Lynd, *The Biggest Bear,* Houghton Mifflin (1953)
Will, *Finders Keepers,* Harcourt, Brace Jovanovich (1952)

Intermediate (Newbery Medal Winners)

Armstrong, William, *Sounder,* Harper & Row (1970)
Byars, Betsy, *Summer of the Swans,* Viking (1971)
DeAngeli, Marguerite, *The Door in the Wall,* Doubleday (1950)
DuBois, William Pene, *The Twenty-One Balloons,* Viking (1948)
Fox, Paula, *The Slave Dancer,* Bradbury (1974)
George, Jean Craighead, *Julie of the Wolves,* Harper & Row (1973)
Henry, Marguerite, *King of the Wind,* Rand McNally (1949)
Hunt, Irene, *Up a Road Slowly,* Follett (1967)
Keith, Harold, *Rifles for Watie,* Crowell (1958)
Konigsburg, E.L., *From the Mixed-Up Files of Mrs. Basil E. Frankweiler,* Atheneum (1968)
Krumgold, Joseph, *And Now Miguel,* Crowell (1954)
L'Engle, Madeleine, *A Wrinkle in Time,* Farrar (1963)
Lenski, Lois, *Strawberry Girl,* Lippincott (1946)
Neville, Emily, *It's Like This, Cat,* Harper & Row (1964)
O'Dell, Scott, *Island of the Blue Dolphins,* Houghton Mifflin (1961)
Sorensen, Virginia, *Miracles on Maple Hill,* Harcourt, Brace Jovanovich (1957)
Speare, Elizabeth George, *The Bronze Bow,* Houghton Mifflin (1962)
Sperry, Armstong, *Call It Courage,* Macmillan (1941)
Wojciechowska, Maia, *Shadow of a Bull,* Atheneum (1965)
Yates, Elizabeth, *Amos Fortune, Free Man,* Dutton (1951)

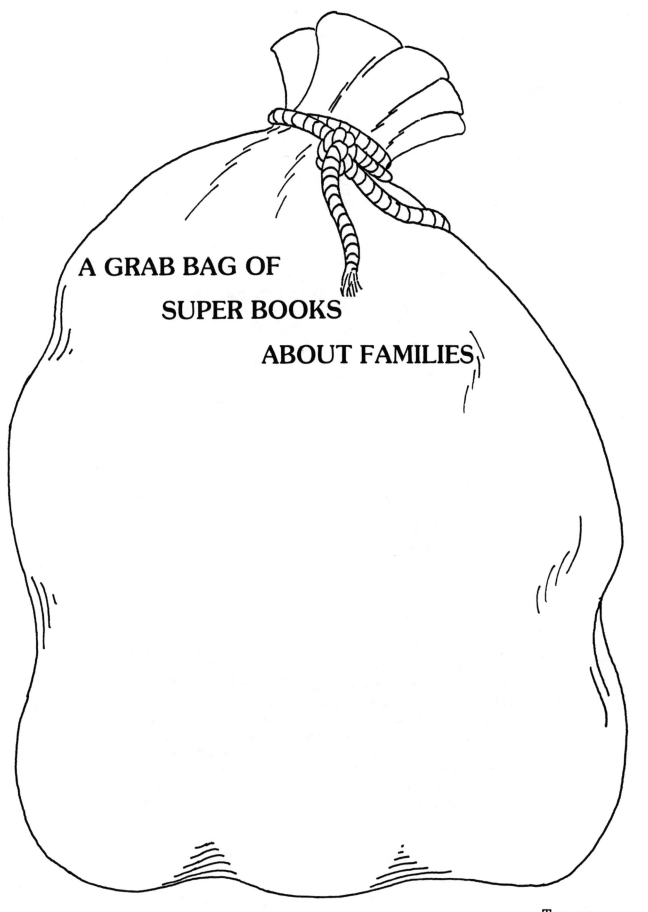

Library Interest-Rousers

Primary

Adams, Florence, *Mushy Eggs*, Putnam (1973)
Alexander, Martha, *Nobody Asked Me If I Wanted a Baby Sister*, Dial (1971)
Caines, Jeannette, *Abby*, Harper & Row (1973)
Hoban, Russell, *A Baby Sister for Frances*, Harper & Row (1964)
Hoban, Russell, *The Little Brute Family*, Macmillan (1966)
Keats, Ezra Jack, *Peter's Chair*, Harper & Row (1967)
Kraus, Robert, *Big Brother*, Parents (1973)
Kraus, Robert, *Leo the Late Bloomer*, Dutton (1973)
Lexau, Joan, *Me Day*, Dial (1971)
Miles, Miska, *Aaron's Door*, Little, Brown (1977)
Newfield, Marcia, *A Book for Jodan*, Atheneum (1975)
Schlein, Miriam, *The Way Mothers Are*, Whitman (1963)
Sonneborn, Ruth, *Friday Night Is Papa Night*, Viking (1970)
Steptoe, John, *Stevie*, Harper & Row (1969)
Terris, Susan, *Amanda the Panda and the Redhead*, Doubleday (1975)
Van Leeuwen, Jean, *Tales of Oliver Pig*, Dial (1979)
Viorst, Judith, *I'll Fix Anthony*, Harper & Row (1969)
Zolotow, Charlotte, *A Father Like That*, Harper & Row (1971)

Intermediate

Allard, Harry, *The Stupids Step Out*, Houghton Mifflin (1974)
Baldwin, Anne Norris, *Jenny's Revenge*, Four Winds (1974)
Bartch, Marian R., *Good Old Ernie*, Carlton (1978)
Blue, Rose, *A Month of Sundays*, Watts (1972)
Brink, Carol Ryrie, *Family Sabbatical*, Viking (1956)
Byars, Betsy, *The Pinballs*, Harper & Row (1977)
Cleary, Beverly, *Ramona and Her Father*, Morrow (1977)
Cleaver, Vera and Bill, *Where the Lilies Bloom*, Lippincott (1969)
Colman, Hila, *Nobody Has to Be a Kid Forever*, Crown (1976)
DeAngeli, Marguerite, *Thee Hannah*, Doubleday (1940)
Estes, Eleanor, *The Moffats*, Harcourt, Brace Jovanovich (1968)
Jordan, June, *New Life: New Room*, Crowell (1975)
Lattimore, Eleanor Frances, *Adam's Key*, Morrow (1976)
Lenski, Lois, *Judy's Journey*, Lippincott (1947)
Mann, Peggy, *My Dad Lives in a Downtown Hotel*, Doubleday (1973)
McCloskey, Robert, *One Morning in Maine*, Viking (1952)
Miles, Miska, *Annie and the Old One*, Little, Brown (1971)
Sachs, Marilyn, *Dorrie's Book*, Doubleday (1975)
Shotwell, Louisa R., *Roosevelt Grady*, Collins-World (1963)
Wilder, Laura Ingalls, *The Long Winter*, Harper & Row (1940)

Primary

Adams, Adrienne, *A Woggle of Witches*, Scribner (1971)
Anderson, Lonzo, *The Halloween Party*, Scribner (1974)
Borton, Helen, *Halloween*, Crowell (1965)
Bright, Robert, *Georgie's Halloween*, Doubleday (1971)
Briggs, Raymond, *Father Christmas*, Coward (1973)
Cohen, Miriam, *Bee My Valentine*, Morrow (1978)
Gramatky, Hardie, *Happy's Christmas*, Putnam (1970)
Haywood, Carolyn, *A Christmas Fantasy*, Morrow (1972)
Hays, Wilma Pitchford, *Christmas on the Mayflower*, Coward (1956)
Hays, Wilma Pitchford, *Pilgrim Thanksgiving*, Coward (1965)
Hirsh, Marilyn, *The Hanukkah Story*, Bonim (1977)
Krahn, Fernando, *How Santa Claus Had a Long and Difficult Journey Delivering His Presents*, Longman Young (1971)
Kraus, Robert, *How Spider Saved Halloween*, Parents (1973)
Mendoza, George, *The Christmas Tree Alphabet Book*, World (1971)
Patterson, Lillie, *Halloween*, Garrard (1963)
Seuss, Dr., *How the Grinch Stole Christmas*, Random (1957)
Simon, Norma, *Hanukkah*, Crowell (1966)
Varga, Judy, *Once-a-Year Witch*, Morrow (1973)
Wildsmith, Brian, *The Twelve Days of Christmas*, Watts (1972)

Intermediate

Andersen, Hans Christian, *The Fir Tree*, Harper & Row (1970)
Barth, Edna, *Holly, Reindeer and Colored Lights: The Story of the Christmas Symbols*, Seabury (1971)
Barth, Edna, *Witches, Pumpkins and Grinning Ghosts: The Story of Halloween Symbols*, Seabury (1972)
Caudill, Rebecca, *A Certain Small Shepherd*, Holt, Rinehart & Winston (1965)
Clifton, Lucille, *Everett Anderson's Christmas Coming*, Holt, Rinehart & Winston (1971)
Dalgliesh, Alice, *The 4th of July Story*, Scribner (1956)
Dalgliesh, Alice, *The Thanksgiving Story*, Scribner (1954)
Devlin, Wende and Harry, *Cranberry Thanksgiving*, Parents (1971)
Glovach, Linda, *The Little Witch's Halloween Book*, Prentice-Hall (1975)
Greenfeld, Howard, *Chanukah*, Holt, Rinehart & Winston (1976)
Hoban, Russell, *Emmet Otter's Jug-Band Christmas*, Parents (1971)
McGovern, Ann, *Squeals, Squiggles and Ghostly Giggles*, Four Winds (1973)
Morrow, Betty, *The Story of Hanukkah*, Harvey House (1964)
Raskin, Joseph and Edith, *Ghost and Witches Aplenty*, Lothrop (1973)
Robinson, Barbara, *The Best Christmas Pageant Ever*, Harper & Row (1972)

BOOKS THAT MAKE YOU GIGGLE AND GRIN!

Library Interest-Rousers

Primary

Alexander, Martha, *Nobody Asked Me If I Wanted a Baby Sister,* Dial (1971)
Allard, Harry, *The Stupids Step Out,* Houghton Mifflin (1974)
Byars, Betsy, *Go and Hush the Baby,* Viking (1971)
Hitte, Kathryn, *Boy, Was I Mad,* Parents (1969)
Hoban, Russell, *Dinner at Alberta's,* Crowell (1975)
Joslin, Sesyle, *What Do You Say, Dear?* Addison-Wesley (1958)
Krahn, Fernando, *Who's Seen the Scissors,* Dutton (1975)
Marshall, James, *Four Little Troubles,* Houghton Mifflin (1975)
Raskin, Ellen, *Nothing Ever Happens on My Block,* Atheneum (1971)
Seuss, Dr., *Horton Hatches the Egg,* Random House (1940)
Sharmat, Marjorie, *Goodnight Andrew, Goodnight Craig,* Harper & Row (1969)
Stone, Jon, *The Monster at the End of This Book,* Western (1971)
Tobias, Tobi, *A Day Off,* Putnam (1973)
Viorst, Judith, *Alexander and the Terrible, Horrible, No Good, Very Bad Day,* Atheneum (1972)
Waber, Bernard, *But Names Will Never Hurt Me,* Houghton Mifflin (1976)
Whitney, Alma, *Just Awful,* Addison-Wesley (1971)
Willard, Nancy, *Simple Pictures,* Harcourt Brace Jovanovich (1976)
Zolotow, Charlotte, *Someday,* Harper & Row (1965)

Intermediate

Bartch, Marian, *Good Old Ernie,* Carlton (1978)
Blume, Judy, *Tales of a Fourth Grade Nothing,* Dutton (1972)
Branscum, Robbie, *Three Buckets of Daylight,* Lothrop (1978)
Callen, Larry, *Pinch,* Little, Brown (1975)
Cleary, Beverly, *Ramona the Pest,* Morrow (1968)
Conford, Ellen, *Me and the Terrible Two,* Little, Brown (1974)
Delton, Judy, *Kitty in the Middle,* Houghton Mifflin (1979)
Draper, Cena C., *The Worst Hound Around,* Westminster Press (1979)
Greene, Constance, *Isabelle the Itch,* Viking (1973)
Kalb, Jonah, *The Goof That Won the Pennant,* Houghton Mifflin (1976)
Matthews, Ellen, *The Trouble with Leslie,* Westminster Press (1979)
Naylor, Phyllis Reynolds, *How Lazy Can You Get?* Atheneum (1979)
Peck, Robert, *Soup for President,* Knopf (1978)
Robinson, Barbara, *The Best Christmas Pageant Ever,* Harper & Row (1972)
Rockwell, Thomas, *How to Eat Fried Worms,* Franklin Watts (1973)
Rodgers, Mary, *Freaky Friday,* Harper & Row (1974)
Sachs, Marilyn, *Dorrie's Book,* Doubleday (1976)
Sharmat, Marjorie, *Maggie Marmelstine for President,* Harper & Row (1975)
Silverstein, Shel, *Where the Sidewalk Ends,* Harper & Row (1974)

Books That Weave a Magic Spell of Fantasy!

27

Library Interest-Rousers

Primary

Andersen, Hans Christian, *The Emperor's New Clothes*, Houghton Mifflin (1940)
Brown, Margaret Wise, *The Runaway Bunny*, Harper & Row (1942)
Burton, Virginia Lee, *Mike Mulligan and His Steam Shovel*, Houghton Mifflin (1939)
Daugherty, James, *Andy and the Lion*, Viking (1938)
Hoban, Russell, *The Mouse and His Child*, Harper & Row (1967)
Lionni, Leo, *Fish Is Fish*, Pantheon (1970)
Lionni, Leo, *Frederick*, Pantheon (1967)
Lobel, Arnold, *Frog and Toad Are Friends*, Harper & Row (1970)
McGinley, Phyllis, *The Plain Princess*, Lippincott (1945)
Minarik, Else, *Little Bear*, Harper & Row (1957)
Parish, Peggy, *Amelia Bedelia*, Harper & Row (1963)
Potter, Beatrix, *The Tale of Peter Rabbit*, Warne (1902)
Rey, Hans Auguto, *Curious George*, Houghton Mifflin (1941)
Sendak, Maurice, *Where the Wild Things Are*, Harper & Row (1963)
Seuss, Dr., *The 500 Hats of Bartholomew Cubbins*, Vanguard (1938)
Slobodkin, Louis, *The Amiable Giant*, Macmillan (1955)
Titus, Eve, *Anatole*, McGraw-Hill (1956)
Waber, Bernard, *You Look Ridiculous Said the Rhinoceros to the Hippopotamus*, Houghton Mifflin (1966)
Williams, Margery, *The Velveteen Rabbit*, Doubleday (1958)
Zolotow, Charlotte, *Mr. Rabbit and the Lovely Present*, Harper & Row (1962)

Intermediate

Aiken, Joan, *The Wolves of Willoughby Chase*, Doubleday (1963)
Alexander, Lloyd, *The Black Cauldron*, Holt, Rinehart & Winston (1965)
Atwater, Richard and Florence, *Mr. Popper's Penguins*, Little, Brown (1938)
Baum, L. Frank, *The Wizard of Oz*, World (1972)
Butterworth, Oliver, *The Enormous Egg*, Little, Brown (1956)
Cameron, Eleanor, *The Court of the Stone Children*, Dutton (1973)
Cleary, Beverly, *The Mouse and the Motorcycle*, Morrow (1965)
Cooper, Susan, *The Dark Is Rising*, Atheneum (1973)
Dahl, Roald, *The Magic Finger*, Harper & Row (1966)
DuBois, William Pene, *The Twenty-One Balloons*, Viking (1947)
Lawson, Robert, *Rabbit Hill*, Viking (1944)
L'Engle, Madeleine, *A Wrinkle in Time*, Farrar, Straus and Giroux (1962)
Lindgren, Astrid, *Pippi Longstocking*, Viking (1950)
MacGregor, Ellen, *Miss Pickerell Goes to Mars*, McGraw-Hill (1951)
Norton, Mary, *The Borrowers*, Harcourt Brace Jovanovich (1953)
Rodgers, Mary, *Freaky Friday*, Harper & Row (1972)
Sauer, Julia, *Fog Magic*, Viking (1943)
Selden, George, *The Cricket in Times Square*, Farrar, Straus and Giroux (1960)
Steele, Mary Q., *Journey Outside*, Viking (1969)
Tolkien, J.R., *The Hobbit*, Houghton Mifflin (1938)

A BASKET OF BEAUTIFUL INFORMATIONAL BOOKS

Library Interest-Rousers

Primary

Aliki, *The Story of William Penn,* Prentice-Hall (1964)
Bartram, Robert, *Fishing for Sunfish,* Lippincott (1978)
Baylor, Byrd, *When Clay Sings,* Scribner (1972)
Busch, Phyllis, *Cactus in the Desert,* Crowell (1979)
D'Aulaire, Ingre & Edgar, *Buffalo Bill,* Doubleday (1952)
DePaolo, Tomie, *Charlie Needs a Cloak,* Prentice-Hall (1974)
DePaolo, Tomie, *The Kids' Cat Book,* Holiday (1979)
Freschet, Bernice, *Moose Baby,* Putnam (1979)
Gibbons, Gail, *Clocks and How They Go,* Crowell (1979)
Goudey, Alice E., *Houses from the Sea,* Scribner (1959)
Hoban, Tana, *Shapes and Things,* Macmillan (1970)
Krementz, Jill, *A Very Young Circus Flyer,* Knopf (1979)
McMillan, Bruce, *Apples: How They Grow,* Houghton Mifflin (1979)
Monjo, F.N., *Poor Richard in France,* Holt, Rinehart & Winston (1973)
Pine, Tillie and Joseph Levine, *Measurements and How We Use Them,* McGraw-Hill (1974)
Rockwell, Anne, *The Toolbox,* Macmillan (1971)
Siberell, Anne, *Houses: Shelters from Prehistoric Times to Today,* Holt, Rinehart & Winston (1979)
Stevens, Carla, *Insect Pets,* Greenwillow (1978)
Tresselt, Alvin, *How Far Is Far,* Parents (1964)
Weber, Alfons, *Elizabeth Gets Well,* Crowell (1970)

Intermediate

Adkins, Jan, *How a House Happens,* Walker (1972)
Aliki, *Mummies Made in Egypt,* Crowell (1979)
Ambros, Victor G., *Horses in Battle,* Oxford (1978)
Daugherty, James, *Daniel Boone,* Viking (1939)
Davis, Bette J., *Winter Buds,* Lothrop (1973)
Faulkner, Margaret, *I Skate,* Little, Brown (1979)
Fine, Joan, *I Carve Stone,* Crowell (1979)
Fisher, Leonard Everett, *The Railroads,* Holiday (1979)
Glubok, Shirley, *The Art of the Comic Strip,* Macmillan (1979)
Greenfield, Eloise, *Rosa Parks,* Crowell (1973)
LeShan, Eda, *What Makes Me Feel This Way,* Macmillan (1972)
Marston, Hope Irvin, *Big Rigs,* Dodd (1980)
McNeer, May, *America's Abraham Lincoln,* Houghton Mifflin (1957)
Norvell, Flo Ann Edley, *The Great Big Box Book,* Crowell (1979)
Phelan, Mary Kay, *The Story of the Louisiana Purchase,* Crowell (1979)
Porell, Bruce, *Digging the Past,* Addison-Wesley (1979)
Poynter, Margaret, *Gold Rush! The Yukon Stampede of 1898,* Atheneum (1979)
Price, Christine, *Dance on the Dusty Earth,* Scribner (1979)
Veglahn, Nancy, *Dance of the Planets,* Coward (1979)
Webster, David, *Track Watching,* Franklin Watts (1972)

BOOKS TO MAKE YOU SHUDDER

CAUTION: Do not read these books before you go to bed!

Intermediate

Aiken, Joan, *Black Hearts in Battersea,* Doubleday (1964)
Babbitt, Natalie, *Knee Knock Rise,* Farrar, Straus & Giroux (1970)
Bauden, Nina, The Witch's Daughter, Lippincott (1966)
Bova, Ben, *City of Darkness,* Scribner (1976)
Branscum, Robbie, *Me and Jim Luke,* Doubleday (1971)
Christopher, John, *Pool of Fire,* Macmillan (1975)
Clapp, Patricia, *Jane-Emily,* Lothrop (1969)
Corbett, Scott, *Take a Number,* Dutton (1974)
Dickinson, Peter, *The Gift,* Little, Brown (1974)
Eldridge, Roger, *The Shadow of the Gloom-World,* Dutton (1978)
Gage, Wilson, *The Secret of Crossbone Hill,* Washington Square Press (1969)
Garfield, Leon, *Mister Corbett's Ghost,* Pantheon (1968)
Hamilton, Virginia, *House of Dies Drear,* Macmillan (1968)
Hunter, Mollie, *The Haunted Mountain,* Harper & Row (1972)
Hunter, Mollie, *A Stranger Came Ashore,* Harper & Row (1975)
Leigh, Bill, *The Far Side of Fear,* Viking (1978)
Poole, Josephine, *Moon Eyes,* Little, Brown (1967)
Prelutshy, Jack, *Nightmares: Poems to Trouble Your Sleep,* Greenwillow (1976)
Preussler, Otfried, *The Satanic Mill,* Macmillan (1973)
Sleator, William, *Blackbriar,* Dutton (1972)

PASS THE POETRY PLEASE!

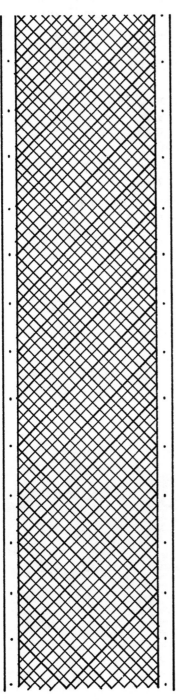

Library Interest-Rousers

Primary-Intermediate

Baylor, Byrd, *Plink Plink Plink,* Houghton Mifflin (1971)
Ciardi, John, *I Met a Man,* Houghton Mifflin (1961)
Ciardi, John, *You Read to Me, I'll Read to You,* Lippincott (1962)
Cole, William (ed), *An Arkful of Animals,* Houghton Mifflin (1978)
Cole, William (ed.), *Beastly Boys and Ghastly Girls,* Collins (1964)
Dickinson, Emily, *I'm Nobody! Who Are You?* Stemmer House (1978)
Ernest, Edward (ed), *The Kate Greenaway Treasury,* Collins (1978)
Greenfield, Eloise, *Honey, I Love: And Other Love Poems,* Crowell (1972)
Hoberman, Ann, *A House Is a House for Me,* Viking (1978)
Hopkins, Lee Bennett (ed.), *Me,* Seabury (1970)
Kuskin, Karla, *Any Me I Want to Be,* Harper & Row (1972)
Lee, Dennis, *Garbage Delight,* Houghton Mifflin (1978)
Merriam, Eve, *Catch a Little Rhyme,* Atheneum (1967)
Morrison, Lillian, *The Sidewalk Racer,* Lothrop (1977)
O'Neill, Mary, *Hailstones and Halibut Bones,* Doubleday (1961)
O'Neill, Mary, *People I'd Like to Keep,* Doubleday (1964)
Prelutsky, Jack, *The Mean Old Mean Hyena,* Greenwillow (1978)
Prelutsky, Jack, *The Queen of Eene,* Greenwillow (1978)
Silverstein, Shel, *Where the Sidewalk Ends,* Harper & Row (1974)
Snyder, Zilpha Keatly, *Today Is Saturday,* Atheneum (1969)
Wallace, Daisy (ed.), *Ghost Poems,* Holiday (1979)
Wallace, Daisy (ed.), *Giant Poems,* Holiday, (1978)
Worth, Valerie, *Still More Small Poems,* Farrar, Straus & Giroux (1978)

Primary

Baker, Betty, *The Pig War*, Harper & Row (1969)
Benchley, Nathaniel, *Sam the Minuteman*, Harper & Row (1969)
Bulla, Clyde Robert, *John Billington, Friend of Squanto*, Crowell (1956)
Coblentz, Catherine, *Martin and Abraham Lincoln*, Childrens Press (1967)
Colver, Anne, *Bread and Butter Indian*, Holt, Rinehart & Winston (1964)
Dalgliesh, Alice, *The Courage of Sarah Noble*, Scribner (1954)
Dalgliesh, Alice, *The Thanksgiving Story*, Scribner (1954)
Gauch, Patricia Lee, *This Time Tempe Wick?* Coward (1965)
Gauch, Patricia Lee, *Thunder at Gettysburg*, Coward (1971)
Lewis, Thomas, *Hill of Fire*, Harper & Row (1971)
Lobel, Arnold, *The Day Peter Stuyvesant Sailed into Town*, Harper & Row (1971)
Mason, Miriam E., *Caroline and Her Kettle Named Maud*, Macmillan (1951)
Monjo, F.N., *The Drinking Gourd*, Harper & Row (1970)
Monjo, F.N., *Indian Summer*, Harper & Row (1968)
Monjo, F.N., *Poor Richard in France*, Holt, Rinehart & Winston (1973)
Parrish, Peggy, *Granny and the Indians*, Macmillan (1969)
Schweitzer, Byrd Baylor, *One Small Blue Bead*, Macmillan (1965)
Turkle, Brinton, *Thy Friend, Obadiah*, Viking (1969)

Intermediate

Baker, Betty, *Walk the World's Rim*, Harper & Row (1965)
Brink, Carol Ryie, *Caddie Woodlawn*, Macmillan (1973)
Burchard, Peter, *Bimby*, Coward-McCann (1968)
Burton, Hester, *Beyond the Weir Bridge*, Crowell (1970)
DeAngeli, Marguerite, *The Door in the Wall*, Doubleday (1949)
Eckert, Allan, *Incident at Hawk's Hill*, Little, Brown (1971)
Fox, Paula, *The Slave Dancer*, Bradbury (1973)
Hickman, Janet, *The Valley of the Shadow*, Macmillan (1974)
Hunt, Irene, *Across Five Aprils*, Follett (1964)
Keith, Harold, *Rifles for Watie*, Crowell (1957)
Lenski, Lois, *Indian Captive: The Story of Mary Jemison*, Lippincott (1941)
Levitin, Sonia, *Journey to America*, Atheneum (1970)
O'Dell, Scott, *Sing Down the Moon*, Houghton Mifflin (1970)
Richter, Conrad, *The Light in the Forest*, Knopf (1953)
Speare, Elizabeth George, *The Witch of Blackbird Pond*, Houghton Mifflin (1957)
Steele, William O., *The Perilous Road*, Harcourt Brace Jovanovich (1958)
Sutcliff, Rosemary, *The Witch's Brat*, Walck (1970)
Treece, Henry, *The Dream Time*, Hawthorn (1968)
Walsh, Jill Paton, *Fireweed*, Farrar, Straus & Giroux (1970)
Wilder, Laura Ingalls, *The Long Winter*, Harper & Row (1940)

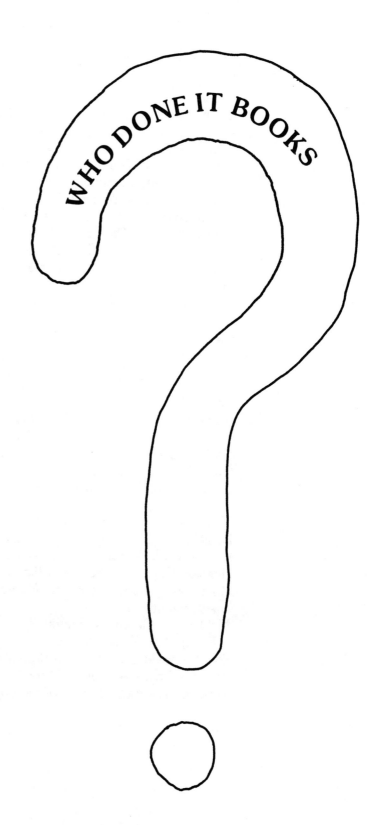

Library Interest-Rousers

Primary

Beach, Carol, *The Tree House Mystery*, Coward, McCann & Geoghegan (1973)
Bonsall, Crosby, *The Case of the Cat's Meow*, Harper & Row (1965)
Bonsall, Crosby, *The Case of the Dumb Bells*, Harper & Row (1966)
Bonsall, Crosby, *The Case of the Hungry Stranger*, Harper & Row (1963)
Bonsall, Crosby, *The Case of the Scaredy Cats*, Harper & Row (1971)
Cohen, Dan, *The Case of the Long-Lost Twin*, Carolrhoda (1979)
Levy, Elizabeth, *Something Queer at the Ball Park*, Delacorte (1975)
Levy, Elizabeth, *Something Queer at the Library*, Delacorte (1977)
Levy, Elizabeth, *Something Queer Is Going On*, Delacorte (1973)
Levy, Elizabeth, *Something Queer on Vacation*, Delacorte (1979)
Lexau, Joan, *The Homework Caper*, Harper & Row (1966)
Lexau, Joan, *The Rooftop Mystery*, Harper & Row (1968)
Myrick, Mildred, *The Secret Three*, Harper & Row (1963)
Rinkoff, Barbara, *The Case of the Stolen Code Book*, Crown (1971)
Shector, Ben, *Inspector Rose*, Harper & Row (1969)
Storr, Catherine, *Lucy*, Prentice-Hall (1968)
Taylor, Mark, *The Case of the Missing Kittens*, Atheneum (1978)

Intermediate

Bauden, Nina, *Squib*, Lippincott (1971)
Bonham, Frank, *Mystery of the Fat Cat*, Dutton (1968)
Bothwell, Jean, *The Mystery Gatepost*, Dial (1964)
Branscum, Robbie, *Me and Jim Luke*, Doubleday (1971)
Corbett, Scott, *The Case of the Silver Skull*, Little, Brown (1974)
Corbett, Scott, *Run for the Money*, Little, Brown (1973)
Gage, Wilson, *The Secret of Indian Mound*, Washington Square Press (1969)
George, Jean, *Who Really Killed Cock Robin*, Dutton (1971)
Hamilton, Virginia, *The House of Dies Drear*, Macmillan (1968)
Hausman, Jim, *Mystery at Sans Souci*, Atheneum (1978)
Hildick, E.W., *The Case of the Phantom Frog*, Macmillan (1979)
Hildick, E.W., *Manhattan Is Missing*, Doubleday (1969)
Holman, Felice, *Elizabeth and the Marsh Mystery*, Macmillan (1966)
Konigsburg, E.M, *From the Mixed-Up Files of Mrs. Basil E. Frankweiler*, Atheneum (1967)
McHargue, Georgess, *Funny Bananas: The Mystery at the Museum*, Holt, Rinehart & Winston (1975)
Sobol, Donald, *Encyclopedia Brown Takes a Case*, Nelson (1973)
Whitney, Phyllis A., *Secret of the Emerald Star*, Westminster (1964)
Wosmek, Frances, *Mystery of the Eagle's Claw*, Westminster (1979)

Library Interest-Rousers

BASKET OF THE BEST

Keep a basket of the best books on a table... make sure to refill it when it gets low!

BOOK JACKET PUZZLES

It's easy to make book jacket puzzles... simply follow these steps!

NOTE: Older children will love to help make these puzzles!

Step One:

Paste a book jacket on a piece of posterboard.

Step Two:

Write a brief motivational statement about the book on the back of the posterboard. For example:

- Do you think all soldiers in the American Revolutionary War were men? You may be surprised. Read *I'm Deborah Sampson* by Patricia Clapp and find out!
- How would you get home if you were swimming in the nude and someone tied rocks to your clothes and threw them in the water? Read *Soup and Me* by Robert Peck and find out!
- Do you think you could survive alone on an iceberg for over two years? Read *The Iceberg Hermit* by Arthur Roth and find out how one boy did just that!
- What would you do if you suddenly found yourself trapped in an underground cavern and an unearthly sound was coming closer and closer? If you're brave enough, read *The House of Dies Drear* by Virginia Hamilton and find out what one young boy did!
- Caution... do not read *Good Old Ernie* by Marian R. Bartch if you are allergic to laughter!

Library Interest-Rousers

Step Three:

Now cut this book jacket apart into puzzle pieces, like this ...

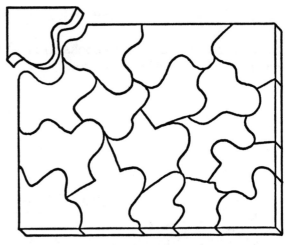

Step Four:

Two other posterboard pieces a little larger than the book jacket puzzle will be needed to do the puzzle. Students put the puzzle together on one of these posterboard pieces. When they are finished, they place the second posterboard piece on top of the puzzle and flip it over. Then they can read the motivational statement on the back.

A PEACH OF A GOOD BOOK

Find a tree branch and weigh it down in a basket or bucket so that it will stand upright. Now cut "peaches" out of construction paper using the following pattern.

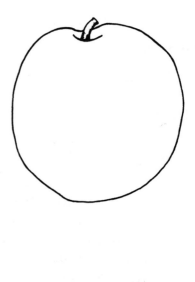

After writing appropriate book titles and authors on these peaches, hang them on the tree. Now make a sign for the basket or bucket that says "Pick a Peach of a Good Book!"

Library Interest-Rousers

WRITE TO YOUR FAVORITE AUTHOR

Have the children write a letter to one of their favorite authors. Often the author will answer! Simply address the envelopes in care of the author's publishing company. Following are some current addresses of the larger publishers of children's books.

> **NOTE:** Be sure to have the children include a self-addressed, stamped envelope.

Atheneum Publishers; 122 East 42nd St.; New York, N.Y. 10017
Bradbury Press, Inc.; 2 Overhill Rd.; Scarsdale, N.Y. 10583
Childrens Press; 1224 West Van Buren St.; Chicago, Ill. 60607
Thomas Y. Crowell Co.; 666 Fifth Ave.; New York, N.Y. 10019
The Dial Press; 1 Dag Hammarskjold Plaza; 245 E. 47th St.; New York, N.Y. 10017
Doubleday & Co.; 277 Park Ave.; New York, N.Y. 10017
Four Winds Press; 50 W. 44th St.; New York, N.Y. 10036
Harper & Row, Publishers; 10 E. 53rd St.; New York, N.Y. 10022
Holt, Rinehart and Winston; 383 Madison Ave.; New York, N.Y. 10017
Houghton Mifflin Co.; 2 Park St.; Boston, Mass. 02107
Little, Brown and Co.; 34 Beacon St.; Boston, Mass. 02106
Macmillan Publishing Co.; 866 Third Ave.; New York, N.Y. 10022
Parents Magazine Press; 52 Vanderbilt Ave.; New York, N.Y. 10017
Prentice-Hall, Inc.; Englewood Cliffs, N.J. 07632
Charles Scribner's Sons; 597 Fifth Ave.; New York, N.Y. 10017
The Viking Press; 625 Madison Ave.; New York, N.Y. 10022

Library Interest-Rousers

BEE IN THE KNOW

A newsletter may be just the thing to create an interest in your library, in addition to its obvious role in disseminating information. Yours could be a one- or two-sheet publication published (on the duplicator) every six or nine weeks.

> **IMPORTANT:** Be sure to include children's work...both drawings and written material. (Various children could be asked to write about new books they have just read.)

You will probably want to run a few of the columns on a regular basis. For example, "From the Librarian" and "Sports Corner" might be in all issues.

For added appeal you might want to run your newsletter on colored paper and place it at strategic points—like a bulletin board—for easy access.

On the next page is an example of a typical library newsletter.

Bee in the Know
Wernert Elementary Library
October Issue #2

A Halloween Poem
by
Robin Pritts
6th Grade

It is orange,
It is black,
I hope I get,
Lots in my sack!

I see ghosts,
I see queens,
It must be,
HALLOWEEN!

Two of my friends,
Nick and Rick,
We got too much,
Now we're SICK!

My Favorite...
by Billy Bartie, 2nd Grade

My favorite book is There's a Nightmare In My Closet by Mercer Mayer. I like it because my dad teases me about a monster being in my closet. When I was real little I thought there was one!
Now my little sister thinks there is a goblin in the basement. I think that is funny. Once I went down and hollered up saying "I am a goblin in the basement and I'm going to get you!" She cried and then I was sorry I did it.

Just In
by Sally Holt, 4th Grade

Here are some new books that you might want to read!
The Stupids Have a Ball by Harry Allard
Three Buckets of Daylight by Robbie Branscum
Absolute Zero by Helen Cresswell
Good Old Ernie by Marian Bartch

Sports Corner

You may want to know more about football! Well, if you do, here are two books that will make you the expert:
Football Talk by Gary Goodby
Run or Pass by Harold Rigsworth

Find the Halloween Words!

```
N B S P O O K T H
G H O S T A R I J
T S K E L E T O N
S W I T C H P K L
B L A C K C A T C
D L S C A R E S O
C O S T U M E H I
J P U M P K I N M
```

From the Librarian

October is a month of goblins, spooks and things that go bump in the night. So, in keeping with the mood of this month, some of your classmates and I have decorated your library for Halloween. You won't want to miss it! See the "terrifying" bulletin board, pick up the monster activity sheet, read a "monster" book and receive a monster badge, read a book in the haunted house, or play the ghost game. Come visit the library if you're not afraid!

© 1981 by The Center for Applied Research in Education, Inc.

Library Interest-Rousers

HANG UP YOUR READING

A fun way to interest children in books *and* decorate your library is with wall hangings. All you need are strips of plain cloth, wooden dowels, glue and string.

Have the children glue wooden dowels to both ends of a strip of cloth. Next tie pieces of string to one of the dowels. The result should look like the illustration.

The children can now illustrate something from a book they just finished on the cloth. Either crayons or felt-tipped pens are good for this art work.

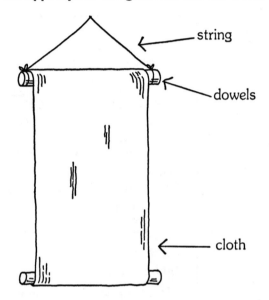

WARNING: If children use felt-tipped pens for the art work, make sure that they place the cloth on top of newspaper, as these pens sometimes bleed through the fabric.

STOP...LOOK...LISTEN!

Arrange a listening post in a corner of your library. A couple of pillows, a play-back tape deck and appropriate books and tapes are all you need. You might want to mount a sign, similar to the one shown below, close to the listening post.

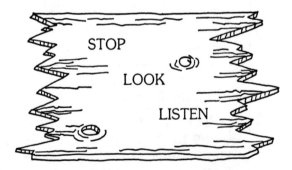

NOTE: Use some of the student-made tapes suggested on page 59 in "This Is a Recording."

Library Interest-Rousers

BE A BOOK PROMOTER!

Provide a space in your library for children to display their favorite books. Explain to your students that, in order to do this, each child must fill out a "Book Promoter Card:"

```
BOOK PROMOTER CARD
You should read _____
_____ by _____
_____ because _____
_____
_____
_____
                    _____
                    (student name)
```

In addition, the child must make something appropriate to display next to the book and card. For example...

```
BOOK PROMOTER CARD
You should read  Charlotte's
   Web         by  E.B.
   White       because  it
  made me cry.

         Judi Baker
```

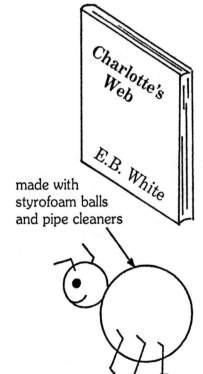

made with styrofoam balls and pipe cleaners

Library Interest-Rousers

Any child who provides a display should receive a "I'm a Book Promoter" button as shown here.

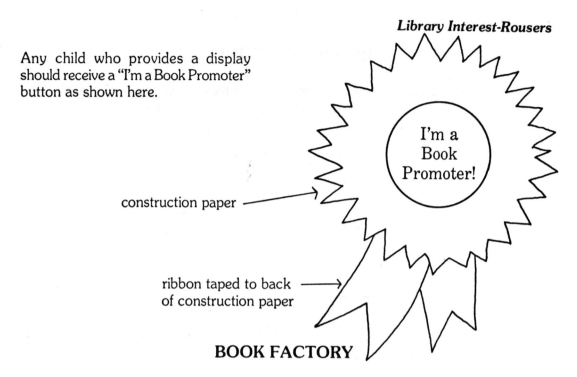

BOOK FACTORY

Encourage children to make story booklets for their own stories. You could arrange a small section of the library just for this purpose. Hang a sign near it declaring it a "book factory!"

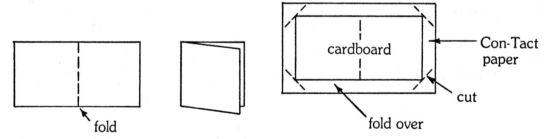

The following materials should be made available in this area: cardboard, Con-Tact paper, construction paper, scissors, glue, stapler, white sheets of paper and felt-tipped pens.

Students may make their own story booklets by following these directions.

1. Fold a piece of cardboard in half like this. Be sure that each half of the cardboard cover is larger than the story pages it will contain.

2. Place a sheet of Con-Tact paper beneath the cardboard. Cut off the corners of the Con-Tact paper as shown here. Then fold the edges of the Con-Tact paper over all four sides of the cardboard.

Library Interest-Rousers

3. Place one of the children's stories between two pieces of construction paper. Then place the story and the construction paper inside the cardboard cover and staple the entire booklet together as shown here.
4. Make a crease in both the front and the back covers, as shown in the illustration above. Now glue the pieces of construction paper to the inside of the cardboard cover.
5. Cut a strip of Con-Tact paper and place it over the spine of the book so that it covers the staples. Trim off the excess.

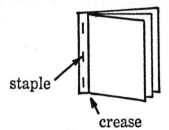

LOCAL AUTHOR'S CORNER

Story booklets made by the children should be placed in a special section of your library, processed in the same way that all library books are processed. That is, cards should be placed in them so that they may be checked out.

SUGGESTION: If time permits, each of these books could also be recorded in the card catalog. This will really add importance to the children's books and encourage participation.

BOOK BAZAAR

Have a periodic sale of children's books made specifically for the bazaar, not those already cataloged and made part of your local author's corner. Children should be able to contribute any of their self-made books and, of course, price the books themselves.

NOTE: Children usually overprice their books at first, but soon discover a "marketable" price!

TERRIFIC TWEETY AWARD

In order to promote an interest in books and reading you might want to organize a "Terrific Tweety Award Program" in your library, classroom, or school. Here is how to go about it.

Library Interest-Rousers

1. Make the bulletin board display shown here. Now duplicate copies of the "Terrific Tweety Nomination Form," on page 49, and place them in the box on the bulletin board.
2. Post signs around your library "promoting" the awards campaign. For example:

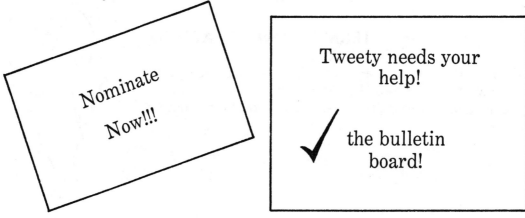

Terrific Tweety Nomination Form

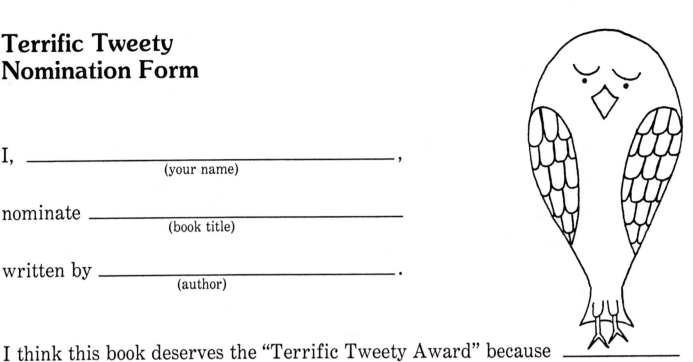

I, _____ ,
       (your name)

nominate _____
              (book title)

written by _____ .
                (author)

I think this book deserves the "Terrific Tweety Award" because _____

_____

_____

_____

_____

_____

_____

_____

_____

_____

Supporters of this nomination are:

    (1) _____

    (2) _____

    (3) _____

    (4) _____

Library Interest-Rousers

IMPORTANT: Each child may nominate only one book and *must* have four supporters' signatures on his/her nomination form!

3. After the time for nominations has passed, select a committee of 4-6 children to review all the nominations. It is their job to determine which eight books will be finalists in the competition.

4. Now, the children who submitted the titles of the eight finalists, with the help of other interested children, must fill out the "campaign booklet form" found on page 51. Simply copy this form on eight duplicator masters and have the children write and draw directly on the masters. Now make ample copies of each of the eight finalists along with the cover page shown on page 52. These should be stapled together to form a booklet.

5. All children should now receive both a "campaign booklet" and an "Official Tweety Ballot." You might wish to use a ballot similar to the one on page 53. The children are then to vote for one book. Now reassemble your committee and have it tally the votes.

6. A program should be planned at which each child who nominated a "finalist" may show his/her book and tell something about it. After this, the results of the election should be announced. Each finalist should receive both a "Terrific Tweety Badge" and a certificate. You may want to use the patterns on page 54.

Book _____

Author _____

Here is a picture of something that happened in this story.

I think this book should win the Terrific Tweety Award because _____

_____

_____

_____

_____

_____

_____

_____

Here are my eight finalists! Read each of them carefully and then vote for the one you like best.

**Official
Tweety
Ballot**

This is to certify that _____

was a finalist in the Terrific Tweety Awards on

_____.

_____
(librarian's signature)

Library Interest-Rousers

MARVELOUS MYSTERIES

Everyone loves a good mystery! Use the following bulletin board and activity sheet to encourage your children to be *Super-Sleuths*!

Activity sheets go in this box.

Name _____

Date _____

I am going to read _____
_____

by _____.

> Now read the first chapter, look at the pictures, chapter headings and book jacket, and then finish this sheet.

This mystery is about _____
_____
_____
_____

I think it (will—will not) be solved because _____
_____
_____
_____
_____

This is what I think will happen in the story:
_____
_____
_____
_____
_____
_____

Library Interest-Rousers

SUPER READER AWARD

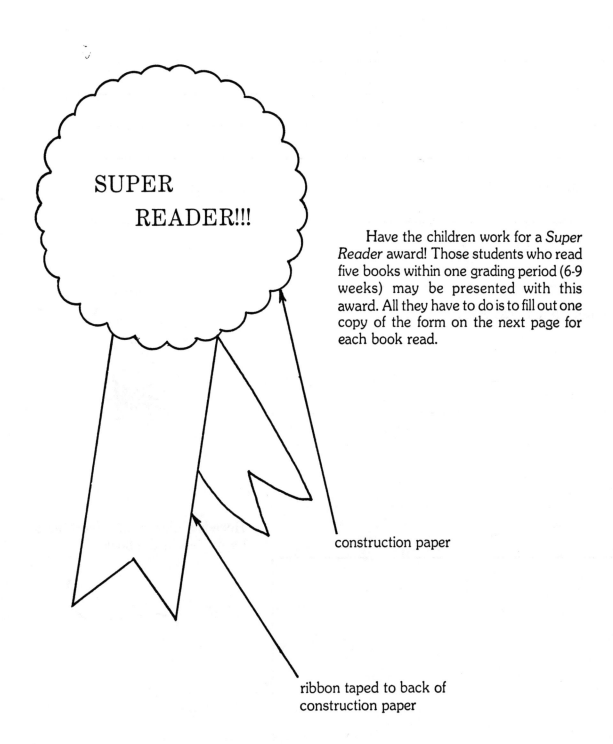

Have the children work for a *Super Reader* award! Those students who read five books within one grading period (6-9 weeks) may be presented with this award. All they have to do is to fill out one copy of the form on the next page for each book read.

Super Reader!

Name _____

Date _____

1. _____ by _____.
It is about _____
_____

2. _____ by _____.
I (liked-disliked) this book because _____
_____.

3. _____ by _____.
My favorite part was when _____
_____

4. _____
by _____.
The character I liked best was _____
_____
because _____
_____
_____.

5. _____
by _____.

© 1981 by The Center for Applied Research in Education, Inc.

Here is a picture of something that happened in the book.

58

Library Interest-Rousers

THIS IS A RECORDING

Create a "recording studio" by cutting and decorating a large cardboard box. Refrigerator boxes are a perfect size! On the inside of one wall, copy the following...

Directions:
1. Choose a book and read it.
2. Read it again, but now plan the sound effects you will need.
3. Read part of the book to the tape recorder. Now play it back. How does it sound? Did you read too fast? Did you read with expression?
4. When you think you are ready, put the sign on the recording studio and begin the taping session.

Be sure to make a warning sign for children to post when they are recording.

If you have extra tapes, why not start a "sound story library," with a play-back tape deck and earphones. This would allow younger children to listen to the story as they "read" the book.

NOTE: If you have a listening center, several children may listen to the story at the same time.

II

Bulletin Boards

The bulletin boards in this section are designed to encourage children to read books from the library media center. Most of them invite children's direct participation.

Each bulletin board suggestion includes a list of materials needed and easy-to-follow directions for constructing the display. The sizes of the materials will depend on your bulletin board space.

Following is a list of the displays with appropriate grade levels for use.

Title	Grade Level
Put on Your Thinking Cap!	primary/low intermediate
Food for Thought	primary/intermediate
Books We Went Buggy Over!	primary/intermediate
Blooming Books	primary/intermediate
If I Were ...	primary/intermediate
Kick Up Your Heels ... and Write a Letter to an Author!	primary/intermediate
Booootiful Books	primary/intermediate
Be an Artist!	primary/intermediate
Funniest Book I Ever Read	primary/intermediate
Children's Book Week	primary/intermediate
Unlock These Doors to Good Reading!	primary/intermediate
Vote for Your Favorite "Little House" Book!	high primary/intermediate
Who Murdered Lady Quackle?	high primary/intermediate
Fabulous Fantasies	high primary/intermediate
Nobel Prize for Literature	intermediate
Books About OUR People!	intermediate

Bulletin Boards

PUT ON YOUR THINKING CAP!

Materials Needed:

    yellow background paper
    black felt-tipped pen
    ditto box
    scissors
    stapler
    tape

Construction Directions:

1. Use an opaque projector to trace the lettering and boy's face on the background paper.
2. Cut the ditto box in half across the width, cover with yellow paper, print "Thinking Cap Sheets" on the front, and attach it to the board.
3. Duplicate copies of the "thinking cap" sheets on page 65, and place a supply in the bulletin board box.
4. Fill out two of the sheets as shown, and attach them to the board.

Bulletin Board Use:

    This bulletin board may be used by primary and low intermediate children. The children are to take a sheet and make up a riddle about one of their favorite story characters. They are also to draw a picture of this character. When finished, they are to return the sheet so you may display it on the bulletin board.

Put on Your Thinking Cap!

I had a bad day.
I lost my marble.
Who am I?

I live in a barn.
My friend is a pig.
Who am I?

Thinking Cap Sheets

Directions:

1. Take a sheet and make up a riddle about one of your favorite story characters. Then draw a picture of him/her.

2. When you have finished, take your sheet to the desk and … your riddle will be hung on the "Thinking Cap" board.

© 1981 by The Center for Applied Research in Education, Inc.

Name _____

Date _____

Directions:
1. Think of one of your favorite story characters.
2. Make up a riddle telling something about him/her. (Look on the board if you need help.)
3. Now draw a picture of him/her.
4. Take this sheet to the desk when you are finished.

RIDDLE:
_____
_____
_____
_____

WHO AM I?

This is a picture of him/her

Bulletin Boards

FOOD FOR THOUGHT

Materials Needed:

    white background paper
    felt-tipped pen (various colors)
    stapler

Construction Directions:

    Use an opaque projector to trace the bulletin board on the background paper. Use appropriate colors for the figures.

Bulletin Board Use:

    This bulletin board may be used to stimulate interest in food and cooking books with primary and intermediate children.

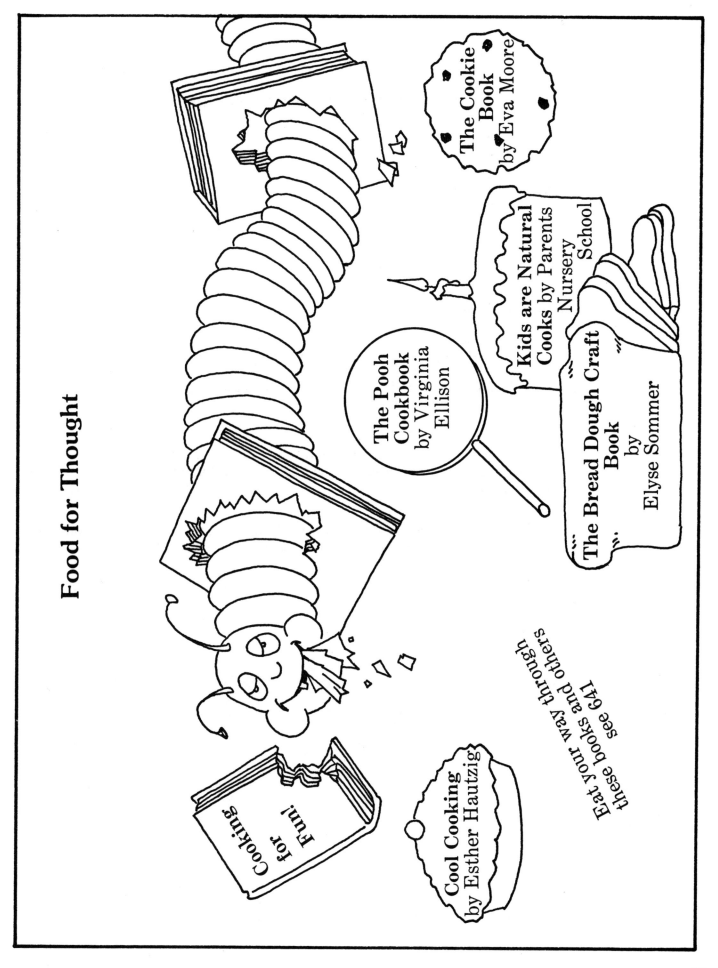

Bulletin Boards

BOOKS WE WENT BUGGY OVER!

Materials Needed:

- white background paper
- green construction paper
- felt-tipped pens (various colors)
- stapler
- scissors
- tape
- ditto box

Construction Directions:

1. Use an opaque projector and copy the lettering and figures onto the background paper. *Do not* copy the two bugs on the tree.

    NOTE: You may prefer to bend pipe cleaners into the shape of the title letters and attach them to the board.

2. Color the tree appropriately.
3. Cut the ditto box in half across the width, cover with the green construction paper, print "Buggy Sheets" on the front and attach it to the bulletin board.
4. Duplicate copies of the "buggy sheets," on page 71, and put a supply in the bulletin board box.
5. Make the bugs using the green construction paper and pipe cleaners, as shown here. Attach them to the tree on the board.

Bulletin Boards

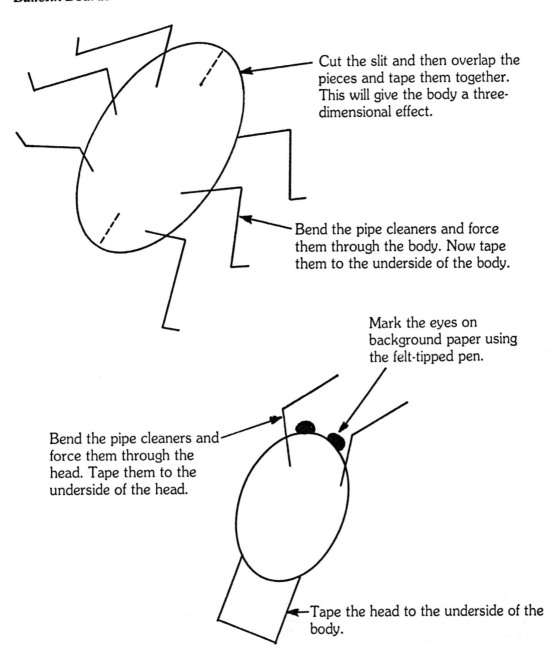

Cut the slit and then overlap the pieces and tape them together. This will give the body a three-dimensional effect.

Bend the pipe cleaners and force them through the body. Now tape them to the underside of the body.

Mark the eyes on background paper using the felt-tipped pen.

Bend the pipe cleaners and force them through the head. Tape them to the underside of the head.

Tape the head to the underside of the body.

Bulletin Board Use:

This bulletin board may be used by primary and intermediate children. The child completes a "buggy sheet" and returns it to you. Display these sheets on the board.

Books We Went Buggy Over!

Directions:

1. Take a sheet and draw a book jacket for one of your favorite books.
2. When you have finished, bring it to the desk and your jacket will be placed on this "Buggy" board!

Buggy Sheets

© 1981 by The Center for Applied Research in Education, Inc.

Name _____

Date _____

Books We Went Buggy Over!

Draw a book jacket for one of your favorite books. When you are finished take it to the desk. It will be placed on the "buggy" board.

Bulletin Boards

BLOOMING BOOKS

Materials Needed:

    white background paper
    construction paper (various colors)
    scissors
    felt-tipped pens (various colors)
    straight pins
    piece of heavy corrugated cardboard
    twine
    two small potted plants

Construction Directions:

1. Cut out 13 tulip shapes from the construction paper and print a letter on each as shown in the bulletin board illustration on page 73. Attach these with straight pins, and then pull the paper away from the board toward the pin heads. This will give a three-dimensional effect.
2. Use an opaque projector and trace the figures and lettering on the background paper. Use appropriate colors for the figures.
3. Make a shelf for the potted plants by using two straight pins, twine, and the piece of corrugated cardboard. (See illustration.)

Bulletin Board Use:

This bulletin board may be used to stimulate interest in books about plants among primary and intermediate children.

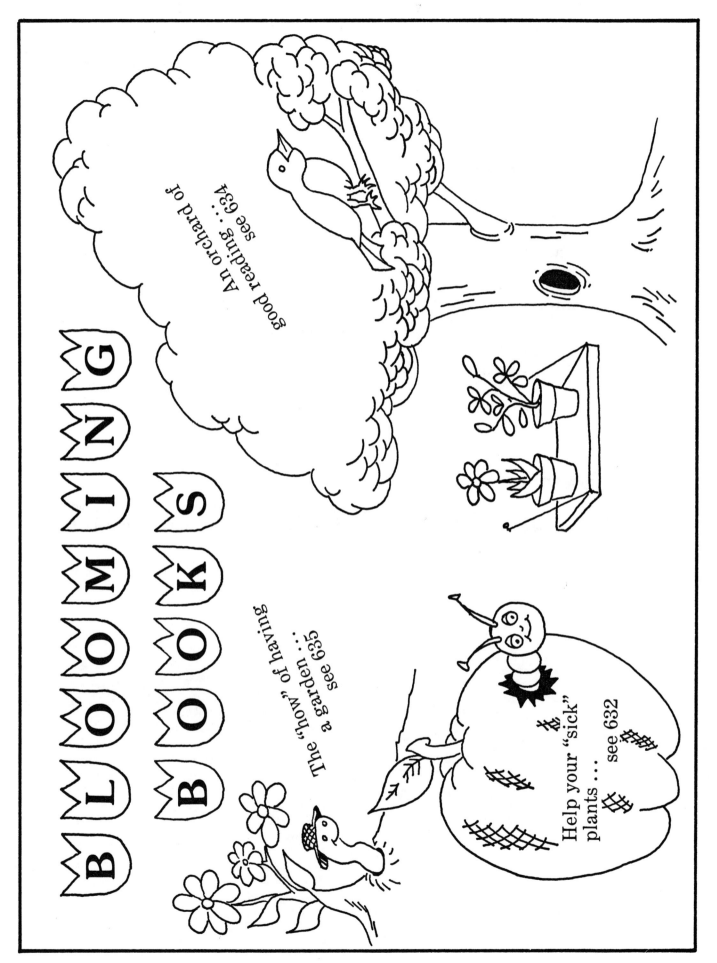

IF I WERE..

Materials Needed:

    blue background paper
    blue construction paper
    felt-tipped pens (various colors)
    ditto box
    scissors
    stapler
    tape

Construction Directions:

1. Use an opaque projector to trace the words and figures of the bulletin board on page 75 on the background paper. The letters should be black and the frog and log in appropriate colors.
2. Cut the ditto box in half across the width, cover with the blue construction paper, print "If I Were ... Sheets" on the front and attach it to the board.
3. Duplicate copies of the "If I Were ..." activity sheet, on page 76, and place a supply in the bulletin board box.

Bulletin Board Use:

This bulletin board may be used by primary and intermediate children. Each child fills in one of the "If I Were ..." sheets and returns it to you. Display these around the library.

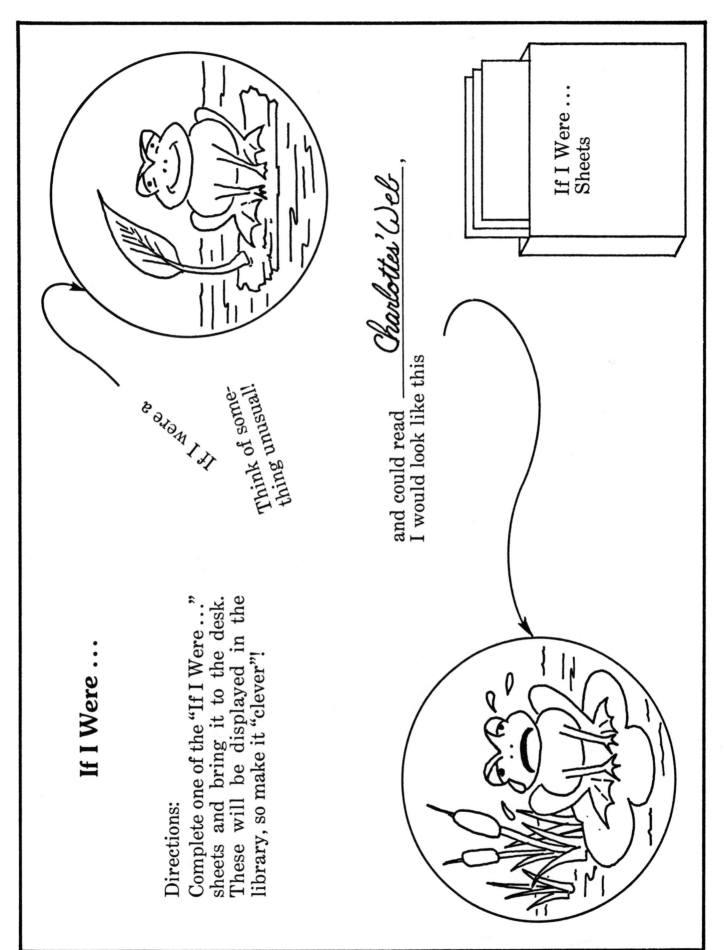

If I Were . . .

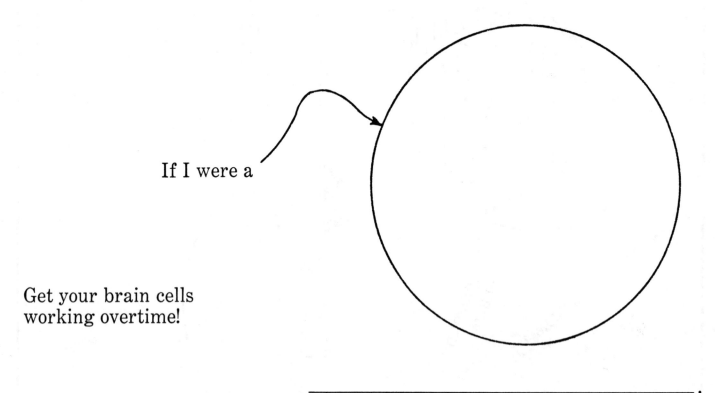

If I were a

Get your brain cells working overtime!

_____,

and could read _____

_____, I would

look like this

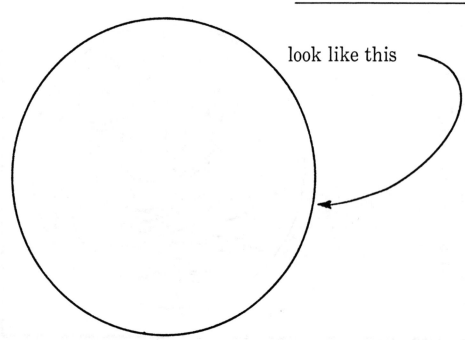

Bulletin Boards

KICK UP YOUR HEELS ...
AND WRITE A LETTER TO AN AUTHOR!

Materials Needed:

green background paper
8 large paper plates
felt-tipped pen
white paper
stapler
gray crayon

Construction Directions:

1. Color the paper plates gray and attach them bottom side away from the board, in the donkey patterns shown in the bulletin board illustration on page 78.
2. Using the felt-tipped pen, finish drawing the donkeys and add the lettering to the board.
3. Print the letter, shown in the illustration, on the white sheet of paper and attach it to the board.

Bulletin Board Use:

This bulletin board may be used with intermediate children. Completed copies of their letters should be attached to the board.

> **NOTE:** You will find a list of the current addresses of major children's book publishers on page 41.

Bulletin Boards

BOOOOTIFUL BOOKS

Materials Needed:

black background paper
white construction paper
ditto box
felt-tipped pen
scissors
stapler
tape

Construction Directions:

1. Cut the letters from the white construction paper and attach them to the bulletin board. You may use the letter patterns provided on page 82 or use other appropriate patterns.
2. Cut the ghosts from white construction paper. Mark them and then attach to the bulletin board as shown in the illustration on page 80.
3. Cut and mark the white construction paper into ghost shapes as shown on page 81.
4. Cut the ditto box in half across the width, cover with construction paper, print "Ghosts" on the front and attach it to the board.

Bulletin Board Use:

The students simply fill in a ghost sheet with a comment about one of their favorite books and return it to you along with the book. Attach the sheets to the board and watch interest grow!

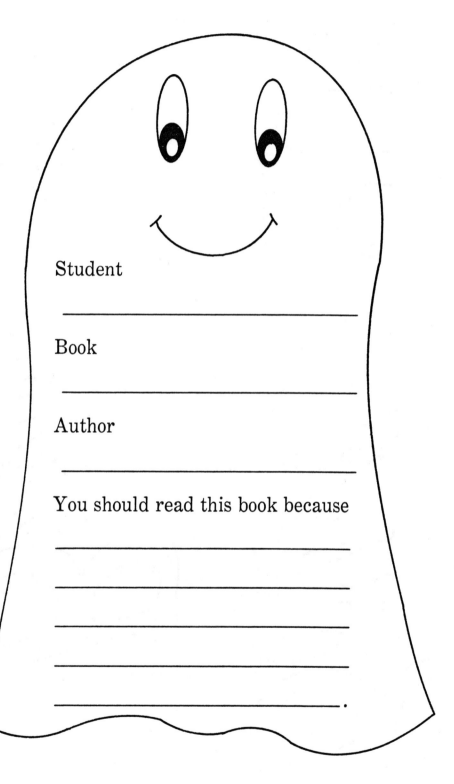

Student
_____

Book
_____

Author
_____

You should read this book because
_____
_____
_____
_____
_____.

© 1981 by The Center for Applied Research in Education, Inc

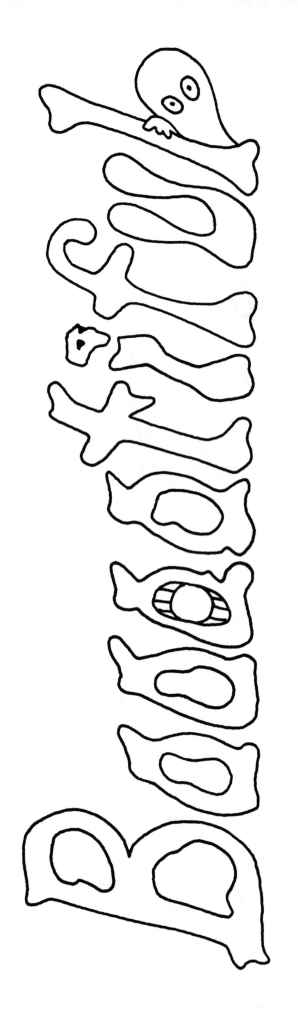
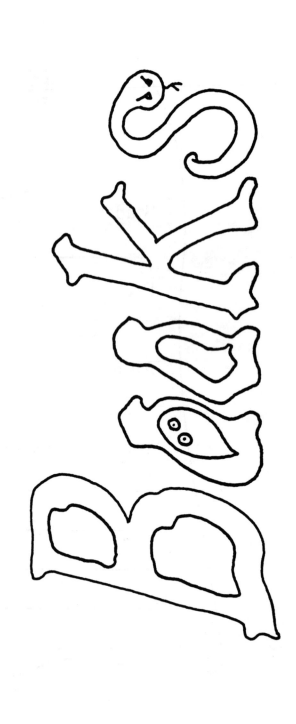

© 1981 by The Center for Applied Research in Education, Inc.

Bulletin Boards

BE AN ARTIST!

Materials Needed:

white background paper
felt-tipped pen

Construction Directions:

Use an opaque projector to trace the bulletin board on the background paper. Use appropriate bright colors for the splotches of paint, artist's easel, brush, and hippo.

Bulletin Board Use:

This bulletin board may be used to stimulate interest in various forms of art among primary and intermediate children.

Be an Artist!

Make your own clay pots. see 738

Learn how to draw animals... see 743

Photographers are also artists! see 770

Become a painter... see 750's

Try your hand at paper folding... see 745

© 1981 by The Center for Applied Research in Education, Inc.

Bulletin Boards

FUNNIEST BOOK I EVER READ

Materials Needed:

red background paper
yellow construction paper circles with 6" diameters
legal-size envelope
felt-tipped pen
stapler

Construction Directions:

1. Use an opaque projector to trace the bulletin board letters and the laughing figure, shown in the illustration, on the background paper.
2. Mark the construction paper circles as shown here.

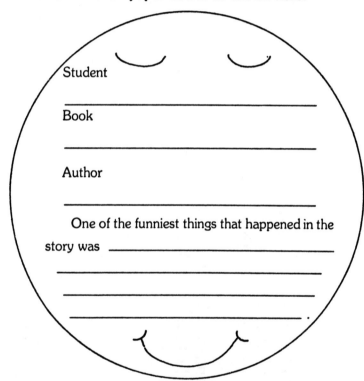

3. Attach the envelope to the bulletin board and draw a face on it.

Bulletin Board Use:

This bulletin board may be used by primary and intermediate children. The students simply fill in a smile face with a description of an incident in their favorite humorous books and return it to you along with the book. Attach these to the board and watch interest grow!

> **SUGGESTION:** You might want to make a tally of the books and set the daily "winner" (the most smile faces) on a table next to the bulletin board.

Funniest Book I Ever Read

Directions:
1. Take a smile face. Tell us about the funniest book you have read.
2. Return it to the desk along with the book.
3. The book with the most smile faces will be declared the "funniest" book in the library.

© 1981 by The Center for Applied Research in Education, Inc.

Bulletin Boards

CHILDREN'S BOOK WEEK

Materials Needed:

    white background paper
    blue tempera paint
    crayons
    permanent black felt-tipped pen
    white construction paper
    stapler
    scissors
    glue

Construction Directions:

1. Use an opaque projector and trace all figures on the white background paper. Using the felt-tipped pen, trace all lettering above the water level, on the clam, and on the trunk.
2. Color the figures on the board making sure to apply a heavy coat of crayon wax (press hard) on each. Make the fish and starfish yellow, the sea plant green, the clam gray, the trunk brown, and the alligator green. *Do not* color over the lettering on the clam and trunk.
3. Dilute the blue tempera paint with water to make a wash. Brush this wash over the area of the board (crayoned figures included) below the water level. This will give an underwater effect.
4. Cut the white construction paper into four signs and copy the phrases, as shown in the bulletin board illustration, on each. Attach these to the bulletin board.

Bulletin Board Use:

    This bulletin board may be used to stimulate interest in reading and the library during Children's Book Week.

Bulletin Boards

UNLOCK THESE DOORS TO GOOD READING!

Materials Needed:

yellow background paper
construction paper—tan, dark brown, and white
three large cereal boxes
five small gelatin or pudding boxes
black felt-tipped pen
scissors
stapler
tape
glue

Construction Directions:

1. Cover the cereal boxes with tan construction paper. Cut the white construction paper and glue to the boxes as shown here.
2. Copy the drawings and information on these "doors" as shown in the bulletin board illustration.
3. Cut a large key out of the dark brown construction paper by using an enlargement of the key pattern shown in the illustration on page 90.
4. Attach the doors and the key to the board. The key should be attached with the small gelatin boxes as backing for a three-dimensional effect. Staple the boxes to the board and then glue the key to these boxes.
5. Copy the bulletin board title onto the yellow background paper.

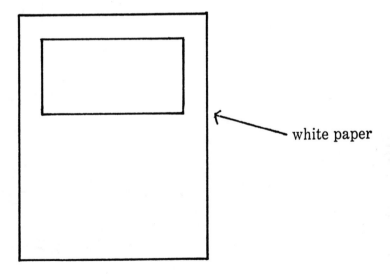

Bulletin Board Use:

Use this bulletin board to stimulate interest in books about travel, sports and animals.

89

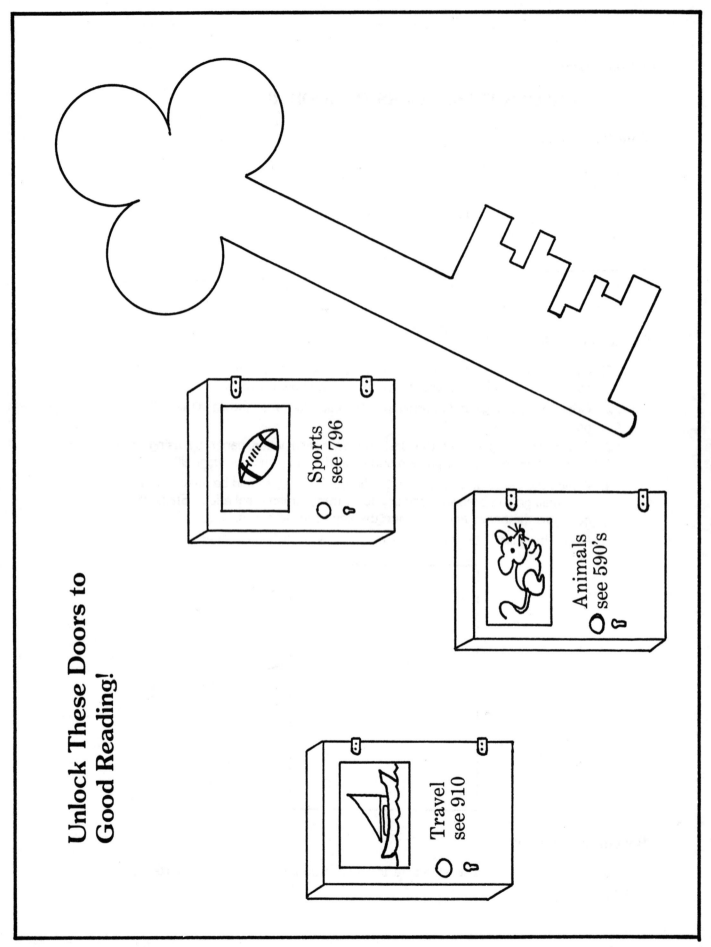

Bulletin Boards

VOTE FOR YOUR FAVORITE "LITTLE HOUSE" BOOK!

Materials Needed:

green background paper
large strip of yellow paper
black felt-tipped pen
ditto box
scissors
stapler
tape
shoe box

Construction Directions:

1. Use an opaque projector to trace the lettering and the map onto the background paper.
2. Cut and roll both ends of the yellow paper to make a scroll. Staple it to the board as shown in the illustration. Now copy the titles on this scroll.
3. Cut the ditto box in half across the width, cover it with yellow paper, print the word "Ballots" on the front and attach it to the board.
4. Duplicate copies of the "Official Little House Ballot" sheets, on page 93, and place a supply in the bulletin board box.
5. Cover the shoe box with yellow paper and cut a large slit through the top. Print "ballot box" on it and place it near the bulletin board.

Bulletin Board Use:

This bulletin board may be used by high primary and intermediate children as they take ballots and vote for their favorite books.

> **SUGGESTION:** The bulletin board display should go up several weeks prior to the voting. Allow only a few days for the voting and post the winner after ballots are counted.

Vote for Your Favorite "Little House" Book!

1. Little House in the Big Woods
2. Farmer Boy
3. Little House on the Prairie
4. On the Banks of Plum Creek
5. By the Shores of Silver Lake
6. The Long Winter
7. Little Town on the Prairie
8. These Happy Golden Years

Directions:
Take *one* ballot and vote. Fold your ballot and place it in the ballot box on the desk.

Ballots

OFFICIAL LITTLE HOUSE BALLOT

Directions: Place an "X" in the box next to the title of your favorite "Little House" book.

☐ Little House in the Big Woods

☐ Farmer Boy

☐ Little House on the Prairie

☐ On the Banks of Plum Creek

☐ By the Shores of Silver Lake

☐ The Long Winter

☐ Little Town on the Prairie

☐ These Happy Golden Years

Bulletin Boards

WHO MURDERED LADY QUACKLE?

Materials Needed:

white background paper stapler
felt-tipped pens (various colors) tape
ditto box blue construction paper
scissors

Construction Directions:

1. Use an opaque projector to trace the words and the figure on the background paper. The letters and puzzle lines should be black and the detective figure in any variety of appropriate colors.
2. Cut the ditto box in half across the width, cover with the blue construction paper, print "Puzzle Sheets" on the front, and attach it to the board.
3. Duplicate copies of the "Who Murdered Lady Quackle?" activity sheet, on page 95, and place a supply in the bulletin board box.

Bulletin Board Use:

This bulletin board may be used by intermediate children. The children take a puzzle sheet and locate the various book titles in the card catalog in order to discover the authors' names. If they fill in the puzzle sheet correctly, the circled letters will spell the identity of the person who murdered Lady Quackle. See the Answer Key below.

ANSWER KEY	
Irene Hun(t)	T
C(h)arlotte	H
Cl(e)aver	E
(B)everly Cleary	B
B(u)rton	U
Arms(t)rong	T
Mary O'Nei(l)	L
Whit(e)	E
Ta(r)o Yashima	R
Ellen Confor(d)	D
Robb(i)e Branscum	I
Scott O' (D)ell	D
Lois Lensk(i)	I
Rober(t) Peck	T

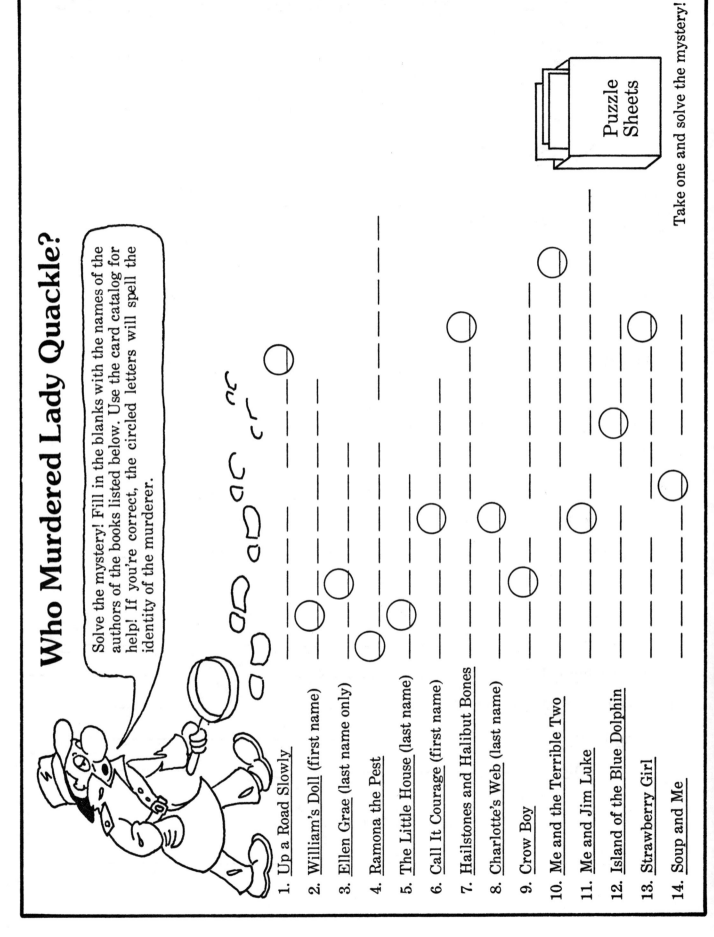

Who Murdered Lady Quackle?

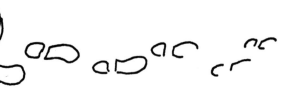

Solve the mystery! Fill in the blanks with the names of the authors of the books listed below. Use the card catalog for help! If you're correct, the circled letters will spell the identity of the murderer.

1. Up a Road Slowly __ __ __ __ __ __ Ⓞ __
2. William's Doll (first name) __Ⓞ__ __ __ __ __ __ __
3. Ellen Grae (last name only) __ __Ⓞ__ __ __ __ __
4. Ramona the Pest Ⓞ__ __ __ __ __ __ __ __
5. The Little House (last name) __ __Ⓞ__ __ __ __
6. Call It Courage (first name) __ __ __ __Ⓞ__ __ __
7. Hailstones and Halibut Bones __ __ __ __ __ __ __ __Ⓞ__
8. Charlotte's Web (last name) __ __ __ __Ⓞ__
9. Crow Boy __ __Ⓞ__ __ __ __ __ __ __
10. Me and the Terrible Two __ __ __ __ __ __ __ __ __Ⓞ
11. Me and Jim Luke __ __ __ __Ⓞ__ __ __ __ __ __
12. Island of the Blue Dolphin __ __ __ __ __ __Ⓞ__ __
13. Strawberry Girl __ __ __ __ __ __Ⓞ__
14. Soup and Me __ __ __ __ __Ⓞ__

Copy circled letters here ↘

__ __ __ __ __ __ __ __ __ __ __ __ __ __

Bulletin Boards

FABULOUS FANTASIES!

Materials Needed:

pink background paper
black felt-tipped pen
construction paper—gray and black
ditto box
scissors
stapler
tape

Construction Directions:

1. Cut and mark the gray construction paper using the castle pattern shown in the bulletin board illustration. Be sure to place the black sheet of construction paper behind the gray sheet and cut them together.
2. Slide the gray sheet down and to the right of the black sheet and attach both sheets to the board. This will add depth to the castle.
3. Use an opaque projector to trace the lettering on the background paper.
4. Cut the ditto box in half across the width, cover with the gray construction paper, print "Fantasy Sheets" on the front and attach it to the board.
5. Duplicate copies of the fantasy sheets, on page 99, and place a supply in the bulletin board box.

Bulletin Board Use:

This bulletin board may be used by high primary and intermediate children. Each child must read a book of fantasy and fill in one of the sheets. Each child who does this may add something to the bulletin board. Just watch the scene expand as the month progresses!

Fabulous Fantasies!

Directions:

1. Read a fairy tale, tall tale, science fiction story, story about animals that talk, or story about an object that acts like a person.
2. Fill in a sheet and return it with the book.
3. Now you may add one item to the castle. It can be anything... windows, flags, trees, dragons, or whatever you wish. Use your brain cells and be creative!

Fantasy Sheets

© 1981 by The Center for Applied Research in Education, Inc.

Fabulous Fantasies

Name _____

Date _____

The book I read is _____
_____

and was written by _____
_____.

It was about _____
_____
_____.

Here are three things that happened in the story that really couldn't happen in real life.

(1) _____
_____

(2) _____
_____

(3) _____
_____

Here is a drawing of one of my favorite characters in the story.

Bulletin Boards

NOBEL PRIZE FOR LITERATURE

Materials Needed:

tan background paper
construction paper—yellow and red
black felt-tipped pen
yellow yarn
scissors
stapler
tape

Construction Directions:

1. Cut out one large badge and eight smaller ones from the yellow construction paper and print the information on each as shown in the illustration.
2. Cut out the ribbons from the red construction paper and tape them on the badges.
3. Attach these pieces to the board along with the yellow yarn. Staple the yarn to the board first and then place the badges over the yarn.
4. Copy the information, as shown in the illustration, on the tan background paper.

Bulletin Board Use:

This bulletin board may be used to stimulate interest in biographies among intermediate children.

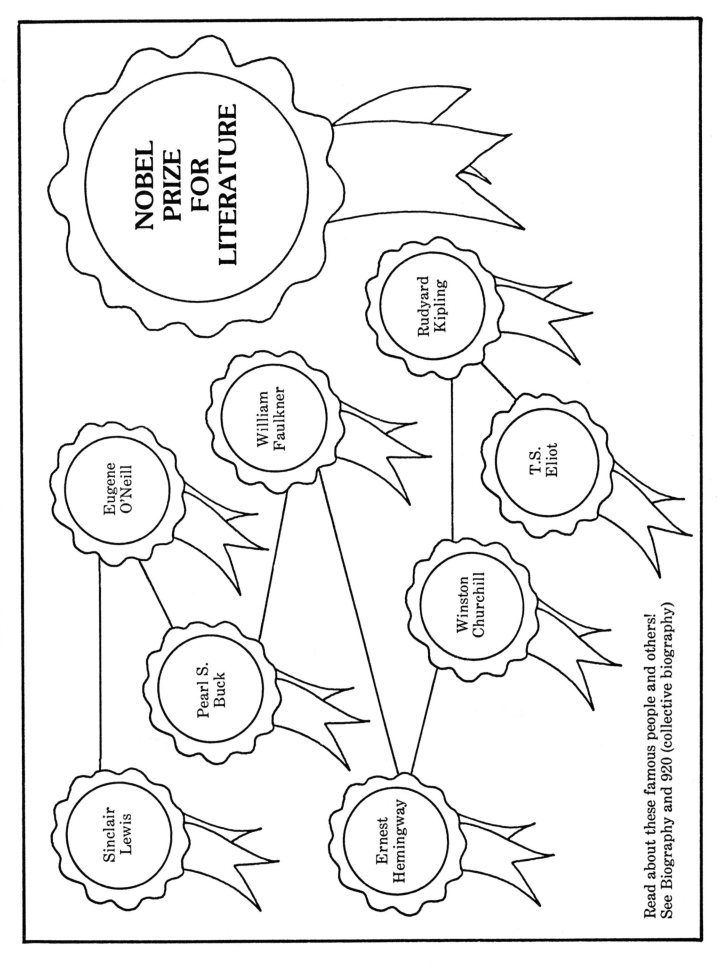

Bulletin Boards

BOOKS ABOUT OUR PEOPLE!

Materials Needed:

yellow background paper
green construction paper
eleven long straight pins
eleven round metal rim tags
legal size envelope
stapler

Construction Directions:

1. Use an opaque projector to trace the map and the lettering on the background paper.
2. Place the straight pins in the map as shown in the illustration.
3. Print each of the following book titles on a different round metal rim tag.

    Shoo-Fly Girl
    Where the Lilies Bloom
    Texas Tomboy
    How Juan Got Home
    Strawberry Girl
    San Francisco Boy

    And Now Miguel
    The Potlatch Family
    Prairie School
    Philip Hall Likes Me
    Bayou Boy

4. Attach the envelope and place the tags in it.
5. Fold the sheet of construction paper and print "Answer Key" on the cover as shown in the illustration. Copy the following on the inside and attach to the board.

    A *The Potlatch Family*
    B *San Francisco Boy*
    C *And Now Miguel*
    D *Prairie School*
    E *Philip Hall Likes Me*
    F *Texas Tomboy*

    G *Bayou Boy*
    H *Where the Lilies Bloom*
    I *Shoo-Fly Girl*
    J *How Juan Got Home*
    K *Strawberry Girl*

Bulletin Board Use:

This bulletin board may be used to stimulate interest in regional stories in our country. It is designed for use with intermediate children.

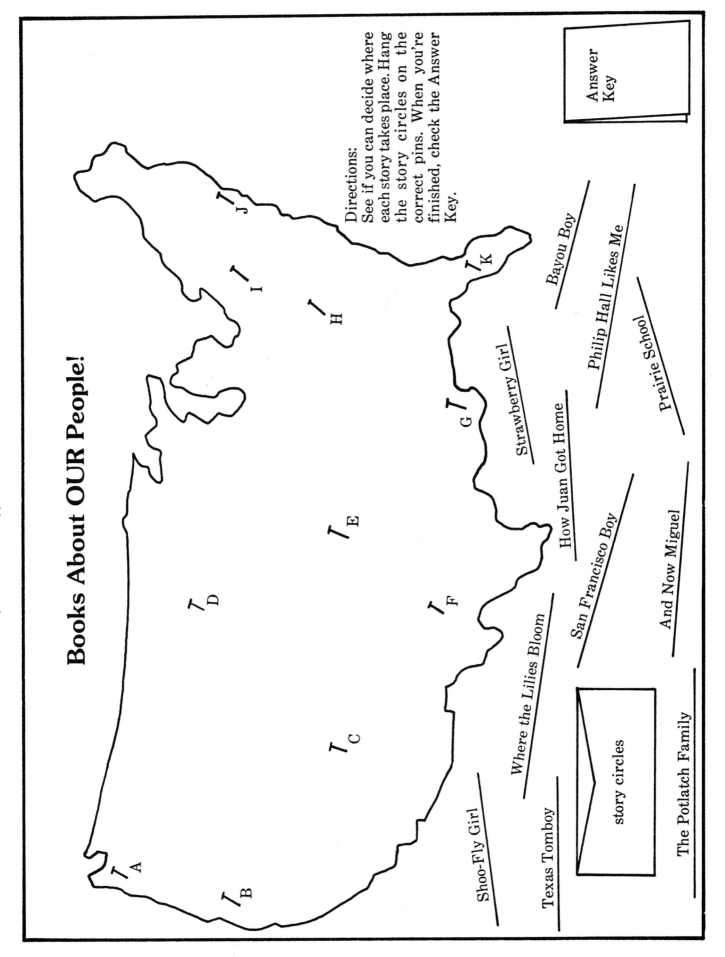

III

Bulletin Board Activities

While bulletin boards help to create an attractive library and stimulate interest in the library collections, these do not have to be their only functions. You can construct bulletin boards that will help you reinforce the library skills you are currently teaching.

This section presents 15 different bulletin boards that reinforce library skills. Each one includes a list of simple materials needed for its construction. The size of the materials will depend on your bulletin board space. You will also find easy-to-follow directions for constructing each display and instructions for using the board to reinforce a specific library skill.

Following is a list of the bulletin board activities, the library skills they reinforce, and the recommended grade levels for use.

Bulletin Board Activities	Library Skill	Grade Level
Candy Factory	alphabetization	primary
Help Robbie Rabbit	distinguishing fiction from nonfiction	primary
Feed the Elephants!	location of fiction books on shelves	primary
Follow the Rainbow	alphabetization	high primary/low intermediate
A Trip to Planet Gleet!	alphabetization	high primary/low intermediate
It's Raining	card catalog usage— subject cards	high primary/ intermediate
Robin's Roost	distinguishing fiction from nonfiction	high primary/ intermediate
Score!	guide word usage	high primary/ intermediate
Sailing	Dewey decimal system classification	intermediate
Surfing!	index usage	intermediate
See How High You Can Fly the Kite	atlas usage	intermediate
Can You Picture This?	encyclopedia usage	intermediate

Bulletin Board Activities	Library Skill	Grade Level
Quacker Questions	table of contents usage	intermediate
A "Monsterous" Vocabulary	dictionary skills	intermediate
Where's the Book?	location of fiction books on shelves	intermediate

Bulletin Board Activities

CANDY FACTORY

Skill Reinforced:

alphabetization

Materials Needed:

white background paper
felt-tipped pens (various colors)
gray construction paper
scissors
stapler
glue

thumb tacks
heavy string
white posterboard
four small gelatin boxes
legal size envelope

Construction Directions:

1. Cut and mark the gray construction paper using the factory pattern in the bulletin board illustration on page 109.
2. Staple the small gelatin boxes to the board and then glue the factory to these. This will give the factory a three-dimensional effect.
3. Use an opaque projector and trace the lettering and figures onto the background paper. Color the figures appropriately.
4. Attach the heavy string to the board with the thumb tacks.
5. Cut and mark the white posterboard using the following candy cane pattern.

Bulletin Board Activities

6. Print each of the following words on a different candy cane as shown above.

ant	dog	go
boy	Ed	house
cat	fast	ink
	Jill	

7. Attach the envelope to the board and place the candy canes in it.
8. Fold a sheet of the gray construction paper. Mark "Answer Key" on the front and the following list of words on the inside. Attach this to the board as shown in the illustration.

    ant
    boy
    cat
    dog
    Ed
    fast
    go
    house
    ink
    Jill

Bulletin Board Activity:

This learning board has been designed for primary children. Children take the candy canes out of the envelope and hook them over the twine in the correct alphabetical order. When they are finished, instruct them to check their order with the Answer Key.

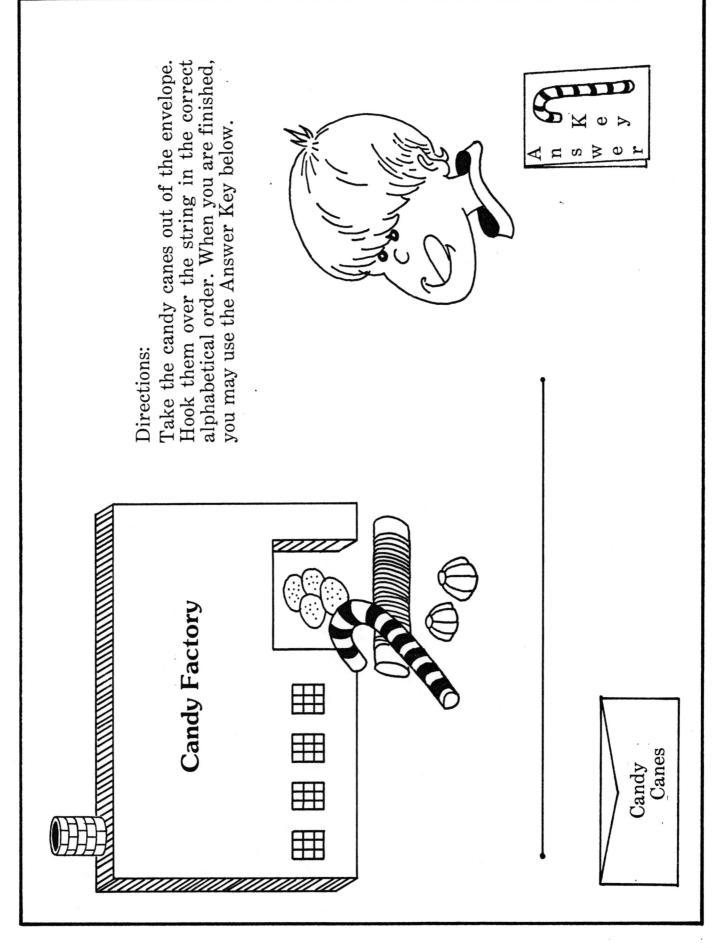

Bulletin Board Activities

HELP ROBBIE RABBIT

Skill Reinforced:

distinguishing fiction from nonfiction

Materials Needed:

white background paper
two bottom halves of cereal boxes
construction paper—brown and white
white posterboard
felt-tipped pens (various colors)
legal size envelope
stapler
scissors
tape

Construction Directions:

1. Use the opaque projector to trace the lettering and the figures in the bulletin board illustration (page 112) on the background paper. Use the felt-tipped pens and color appropriately.
2. Cover the bottom halves of the cereal boxes with brown construction paper, and attach two strips of brown construction paper for handles. Label each as shown in the illustration. Attach the baskets and the labels to the board.
3. Cut and mark the white posterboard pieces in the egg shape shown here.

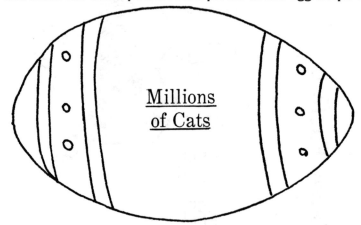

4. Print each of the following book titles on a different egg as shown above.

The Tale of Peter Rabbit *The First Book of Birds*
Make Way for Ducklings *Here Come the Cottontails*
Millions of Cats *Egg-ventures: First Science Experiments*
Blueberries for Sal *A Skyscraper Goes Up*
Once a Mouse *Egg Craft*

Bulletin Board Activities

5. Attach the envelope to the board, print "eggs" on it, and place the eggs in it.
6. Fold the sheet of construction paper, mark the cover as shown in the illustration and the inside as shown below, and attach it to the board.

Fiction	Nonfiction
The Tale of Peter Rabbit	The First Book of Birds
Make Way for Ducklings	Here Come the Cottontails
Millions of Cats	Egg-Ventures: First Science Experiments
Blueberries for Sal	A Skyscraper Goes Up
Once a Mouse	Egg Craft

Bulletin Board Activity:

This learning board may be used by primary children. They are to take the eggs and place them in the appropriate basket, Fiction or Nonfiction. When they are finished they may use the Answer Key.

Help Robbie Rabbit

Help me fill up my baskets with eggs! Follow the directions in the large egg.

1. Take the eggs out of the envelope.
2. Place them in the correct baskets.

REMEMBER:
Books of fiction are made-up stories. Nonfiction books give factual information.

If you need help... use the card catalog.

Answer Key

NONFICTION

FICTION

eggs

© 1981 by The Center for Applied Research in Education, Inc.

Bulletin Board Activities

FEED THE ELEPHANTS!

Skill Reinforced:

location of fiction books on shelves in alphabetical order

Materials Needed:

6 library book card pockets
pink background paper
construction paper—gray and brown
small gelatin boxes
stapler

glue
brown posterboard
black felt-tipped pen
legal size envelope
scissors

Construction Directions:

1. Use an opaque projector and trace the elephant and the lettering in the bulletin board illustration (page 115) on the gray construction paper. Attach the small gelatin boxes to the board and glue the elephant to these. This will give a three-dimensional effect.
2. Cut, mark and letter the brown construction paper into the peanut heading as shown in the upper left-hand corner of the illustration. Attach these to the board.
3. Cut and mark the gray construction paper using the elephant pattern shown here.

Bulletin Board Activities

4. Glue the elephants to the library book card pockets and attach them to the board as shown in the illustration.
5. Cut and mark the brown posterboard using the peanut pattern shown here.

6. Print each of the following authors' names and titles on a different peanut as shown above.

   Madeline by Ludwig Bemelmans
   Chanticleer and the Fox by Barbara Cooney
   Petunia by Roger Duvoisin
   The Happy Lion by Louise Fatio
   Good Night, Owl by Pat Hutchins
   The Snowy Day by Ezra Jack Keats

7. Attach the large envelope to the board and place the peanuts in it.
8. Fold a sheet of the brown construction paper and mark the cover as shown in the illustration.
9. Copy the following on the inside of the "Answer Key" and attach to the board.

   Madeline by Ludwig Bemelmans
   Chanticleer and the Fox by Barbara Cooney
   Petunia by Roger Duvoisin
   The Happy Lion by Louise Fatio
   Good Night, Owl by Pat Hutchins
   The Snowy Day by Ezra Jack Keats

Bulletin Board Activity:

This learning board may be used by children in the high primary grades. They are to place the peanuts from left to right in alphabetical order in the "elephant pockets" as they would expect to find them on the library shelves. When they are finished they may use the Answer Key.

Feed the Elephants!

Directions:
1. Take the peanuts out of the envelope.
2. Place them in the elephant pockets like you would find them on the bookshelves. Hint: Use author's last name!
3. When you finish you may use the Answer Key. Be sure to put the peanuts back.

Answer Key

peanuts

Bulletin Board Activities

FOLLOW THE RAINBOW

Skill Reinforced:

alphabetization

Materials Needed:

white background paper	legal size envelope
straight pins	scissors
felt-tipped pens (various colors)	stapler
gray posterboard	construction paper—yellow and blue

Construction Directions:

1. Use an opaque projector to trace the words, the clouds, the pot-of-gold, and the rainbow in the bulletin board illustration (page 118) on the background paper. Use appropriate colors.
2. Place the straight pins on the board as shown in the illustration.
3. Cut and mark the yellow paper using an enlargement of the following sun pattern. Attach it to the board.

Bulletin Board Activities

4. Cut the gray posterboard using the following pattern.

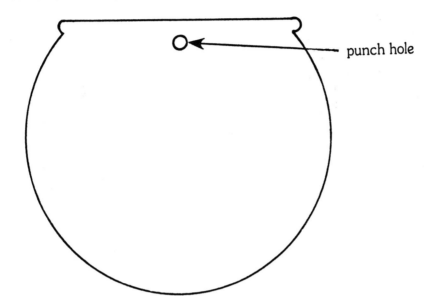

5. Print each of the following words in a different pot-of-gold.

habit	hall
had	hamlet
hail	hammer
hair	hand
half	hang

6. Attach the large envelope to the board and mark "pots-of-gold" on it. Place the pots-of-gold in it.
7. Fold the blue construction paper and mark the cover "Answer Key" as shown in the illustration. Copy the following on the inside and attach to the board.

    1—habit
    2—had
    3—hail
    4—hair
    5—half
    6—hall
    7—hamlet
    8—hammer
    9—hand
    10—hang

Bulletin Board Activity:

This learning board may be used by children in the high primary or low intermediate grades. They are to place the pots-of-gold on the pins in their correct alphabetical order. They may use the Answer Key when finished.

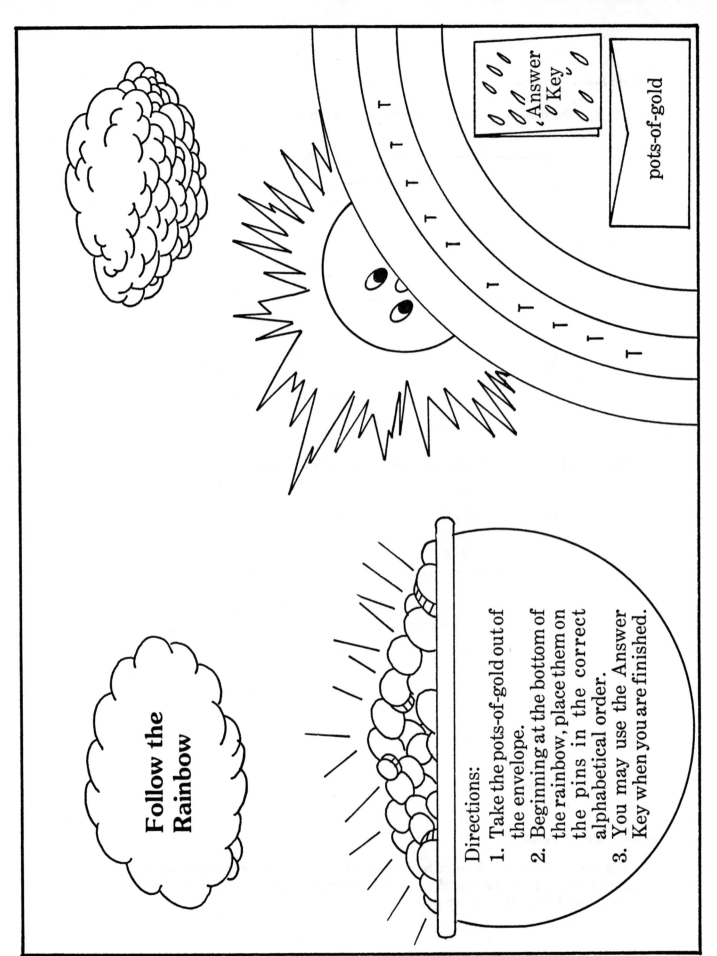

Bulletin Board Activities

A TRIP TO PLANET GLEET!

Skill Reinforced:

alphabetization

Materials Needed:

white background paper
felt-tipped pens (various colors)
legal size envelope
library book card pockets
stapler
posterboard—red, white and blue
scissors

Construction Directions:

1. Use an opaque projector to mark the lettering and figures in the bulletin board illustration (page 121) on the background paper. Use appropriate colors.
2. Number and attach the library book card pockets to the board as shown in the illustration.
3. Cut and mark the red posterboard pieces into rockets as shown here.

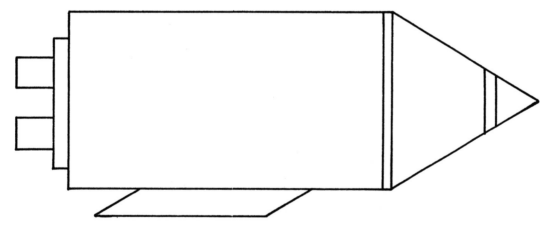

4. Copy each of the following words on a different red rocket.

astronaut	rocket
comet	satellite
launch pad	solar system
meteor	space
planet	star

Bulletin Board Activities

5. Fold and mark the blue posterboard "Answer Key" as shown in the illustration. Copy the following on the inside and attach to the board.

   1—astronaut
   2—comet
   3—launch pad
   4—meteor
   5—planet
   6—rocket
   7—satellite
   8—solar system
   9—space
   10—star

6. Attach the large envelope to the board and mark "rockets" on it. Place the rockets in this envelope.

7. Copy the illustration on page 122 on the white sheet of posterboard and hang it next to the learning board.

Bulletin Board Activity:

This bulletin board may be used by children in the high primary or low intermediate grades. They are to place the rockets into the pockets in their correct alphabetical order. They may use the Answer Key when finished.

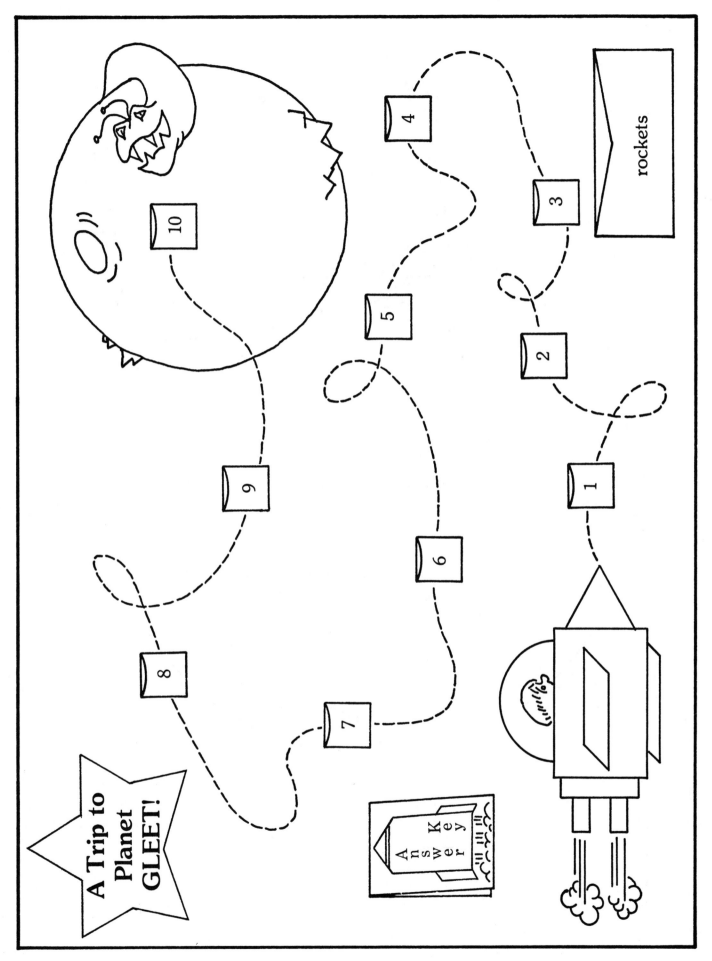

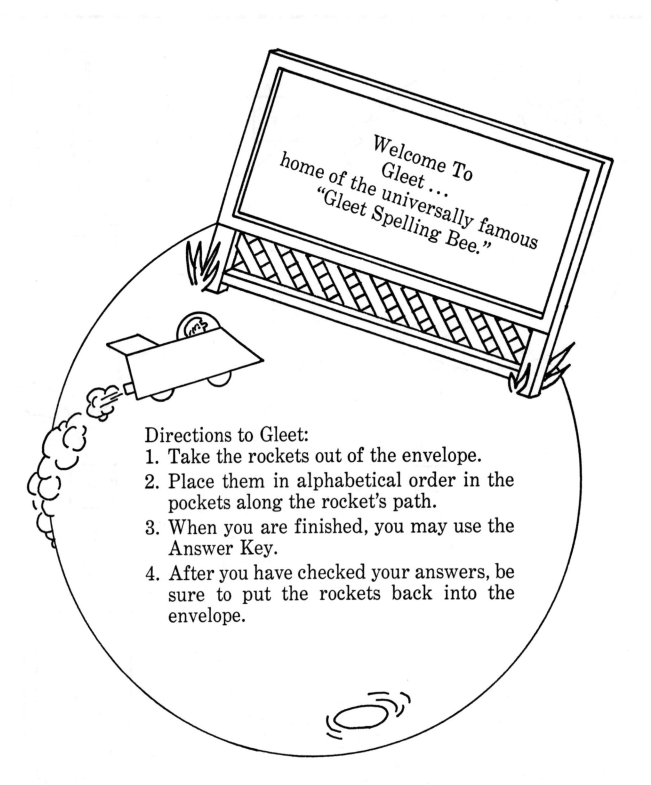

Bulletin Board Activities

IT'S RAINING

Skill Reinforced:

card catalog usage—subject cards

Materials Needed:

blue background paper
white paper
construction paper—red and blue
small gelatin boxes
straight pins
felt-tipped pens (various colors)
legal size envelope
stapler
blue posterboard

Construction Directions:

1. Cut and mark the white paper using the cloud pattern in the bulletin board illustration on page 125. Attach this to the board.
2. Cut and mark the red construction paper using the umbrella pattern in the illustration. Attach the gelatin boxes to the board and glue the umbrella to these. This will give a three-dimensional effect.
3. Use an opaque projector to trace the lettering, raindrops, and umbrella handle onto the background paper.
4. Place straight pins above the guide letters as in the illustration.
5. Cut the blue posterboard pieces using the following raindrop pattern.

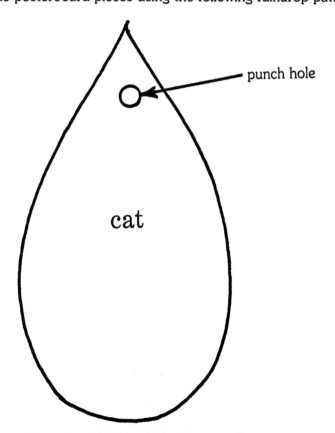

6. Print each of the following guide letters on a different raindrop as shown above.

>   dog
>   cat
>   horse
>   duck
>   pig
>   chicken
>   sheep
>   goat

7. Mark the envelope "raindrops" and attach it to the board. Place the raindrops in it.
8. Fold the blue construction paper and mark the cover "Answer Key" as shown in the illustration. Copy the following and staple it inside the Answer Key.

>   bi–cha   cat
>   che–cum   chicken
>   cun–dos   dog
>   dot–e   duck
>   f–hag   goat
>   hah–k   horse
>   l–rec   pig
>   red–t   sheep

Bulletin Board Activity:

This learning board may be used for children in the high primary and intermediate grades. Children take the raindrops out of the envelope and, according to the guide letters under each pin, hang them correctly. They may use the Answer Key when finished.

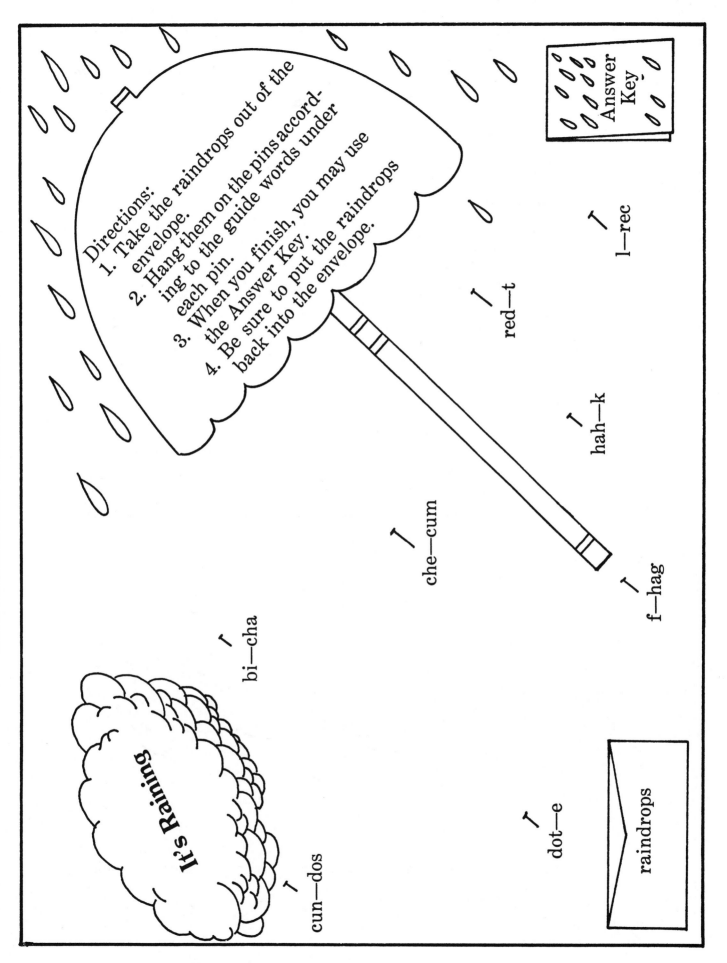

Bulletin Board Activities

ROBIN'S ROOST

Skill Reinforced:

distinguishing fiction from nonfiction

Materials Needed:

white background paper
felt-tipped pens (various colors)
green corrugated paper
brown construction paper
tan posterboard
straight pins
scissors
stapler
legal size envelope

Construction Directions:

1. Cut the green corrugated paper into the treetop shapes, as shown in the bulletin board illustration on page 128, and attach it to the board.
2. Use an opaque projector to trace the lettering and figures on the background paper. Use appropriate colors.
3. Cut and mark the brown construction paper using the following nest pattern.

4. Attach the nests to the board as shown in the illustration and fasten a straight pin in each.

Bulletin Board Activities

5. Cut and mark the tan posterboard using the bird pattern shown here.

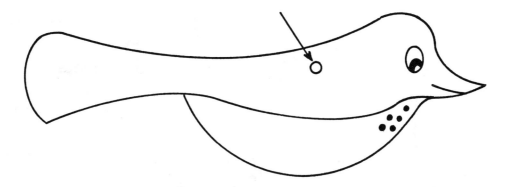

6. Print the following book titles each on a different robin.
    The Borrowers
    The Hobbit
    Charlotte's Web
    Chitty-Chitty-Bang-Bang
    The Magic Finger
    A First Look at Insects
    The Mayflower and the Pilgrim Fathers
    How to Make Your Own Movies
    What Did the Dinosaurs Eat?
    Let's Look at Reptiles

7. Attach the large envelope to the board, mark "robins" on the front, and place the robins in it.

8. Fold a sheet of brown construction paper and mark the front "Answer Key" as shown in the illustration.

9. Print the following on the inside of the Answer Key and attach it to the board.

<u>Fiction</u>	<u>Nonfiction</u>
The Borrowers	*A First Look at Insects*
The Hobbit	*The Mayflower and the Pilgrim Fathers*
Charlotte's Web	
Chitty-Chitty-Bang-Bang	*How to Make Your Own Movies*
The Magic Finger	*What Did the Dinosaurs Eat?*
	Let's Look at Reptiles

Bulletin Board Activity:

This bulletin board is appropriate for the high primary and intermediate grades. The children place the robins on the correct trees: Fiction or Nonfiction. When they are finished they may use the Answer Key.

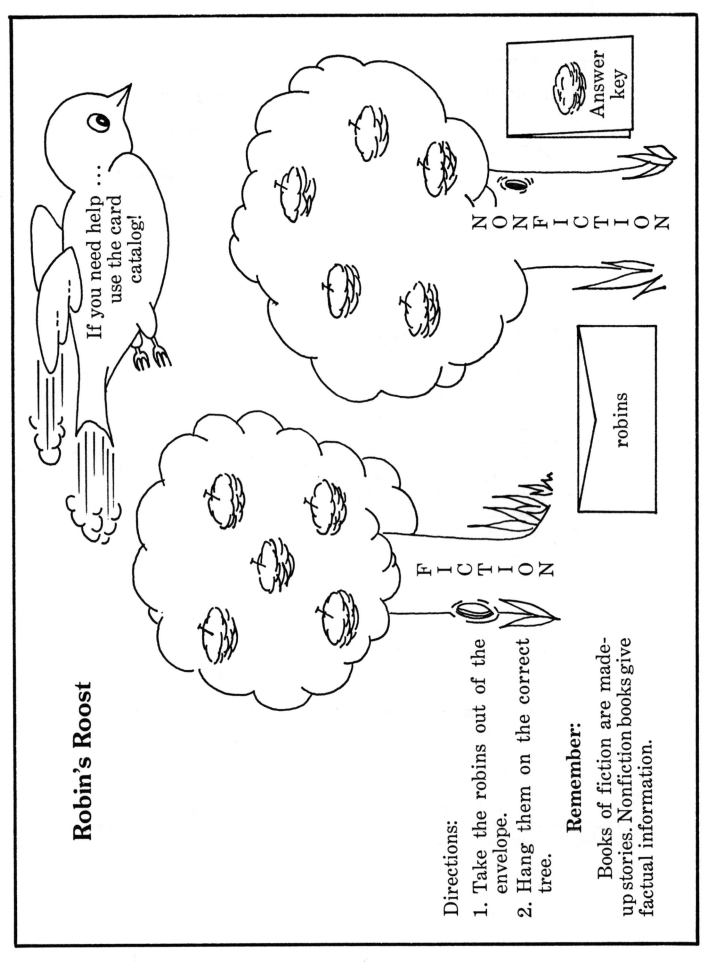

Bulletin Board Activities

SCORE!

Skill Reinforced:

guide word usage

Materials Needed:

white background paper
felt-tipped pens (various colors)
legal size envelope
yellow construction paper

brown posterboard
scissors
straight pins

Construction Directions:

1. Use an opaque projector to trace the lettering and the figures in the bulletin board illustration (page 131) onto the background paper. Color appropriately.
2. Place the straight pins on the board as shown in the illustration.
3. Cut and mark the posterboard using the following basketball pattern.

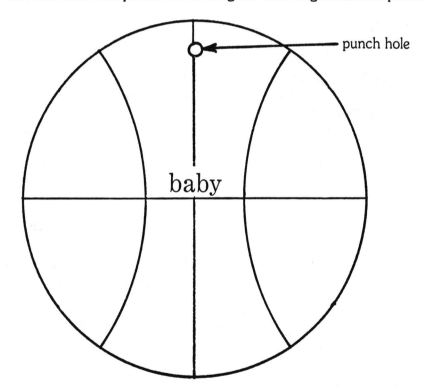

4. Print each of the following words on a different basketball as shown above.

   baby   balance
   bacteria   ballet
   badminton   balmy
   bail   band

129

Bulletin Board Activities

5. Mark and attach the large envelope to the board and place the basketballs in it.
6. Fold the yellow construction paper and mark "Answer Key" on the cover as shown in the illustration. Print the following on the inside of the Answer Key and attach it to the board.

    baboon — back
      baby
    bacon — bad
      bacteria
    badge — bag
      badminton
    baggage — bait
      bail
    bake — bald
      balance
    ball — balloon
      ballet
    ballot — bamboo
      balmy
    banana — bandage
      band

Bulletin Board Activity:

This learning board is for children in the high primary and intermediate grades. Children are to hang the basketballs under their correct guide words. They may use the Answer Key when they are finished.

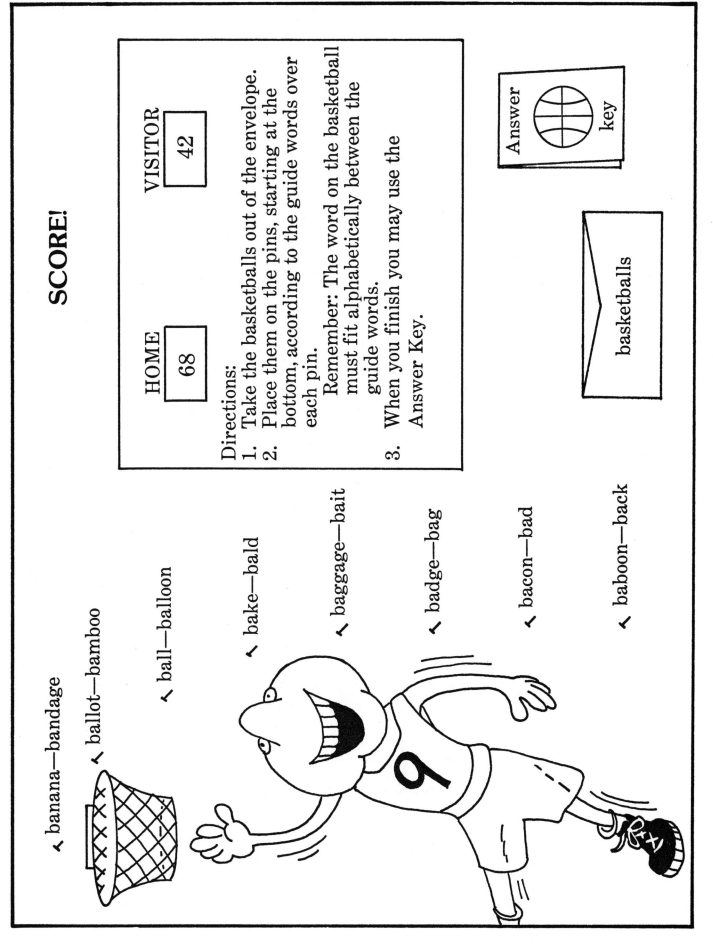

Bulletin Board Activities

SAILING

Skill Reinforced:

Dewey decimal system classification

Materials Needed:

 white background paper
 blue construction paper
 felt-tipped pens (various colors)
 library book card pockets
 stapler
 legal size envelope
 white posterboard
 scissors

Construction Directions:

1. Use an opaque projector to trace the lettering and the figures in the bulletin board illustration (page 134) on the background paper. Color appropriately.
2. Attach the library book card pockets and write the Dewey decimal numerals on them as shown in the illustration.
3. Mark and cut the white posterboard into the following lighthouse pattern. You will need ten.

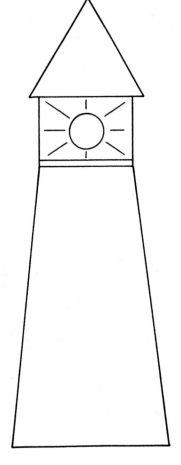

Bulletin Board Activities

4. Write each of the following categories on a different lighthouse.

    Social Sciences   History
    The Arts   Literature
    Religion   General Works
    Philosophy   Language
    Pure Science   Technology

5. Fold the blue construction paper and mark the cover "Answer Key" as shown in the illustration. Copy the following on the inside and attach it to the board.

    000-099   General Works
    100-199   Philosophy
    200-299   Religion
    300-399   Social Sciences
    400-499   Language
    500-599   Pure Science
    600-699   Technology
    700-799   The Arts
    800-899   Literature
    900-999   History

6. Attach the envelope to the bulletin board and place the lighthouses in it.

Bulletin Board Activity:

This learning board may be used by children in the intermediate grades. Children take the lighthouses from the envelope and attempt to place them in the pockets whose numerals correspond to the category written on the lighthouse. Students can check their work by looking at the Answer Key.

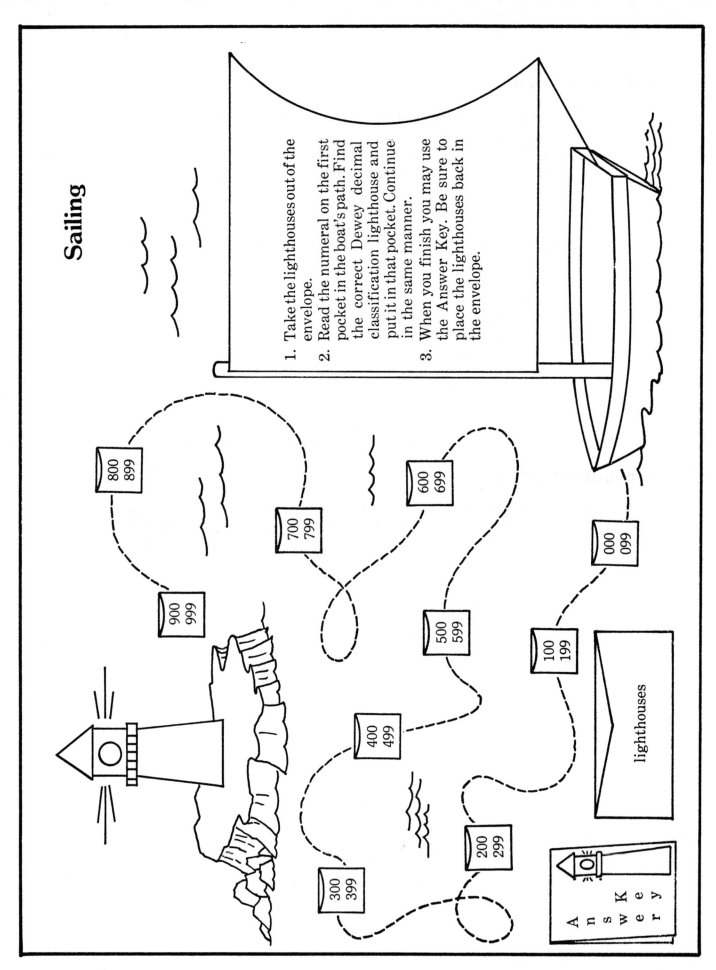

Bulletin Board Activities

SURFING!

Skill Reinforced:

index usage

Materials Needed:

white background paper
library book card pockets
felt-tipped pens (various colors)
stapler
scissors
brown posterboard
blue construction paper
legal size envelope

Construction Directions:

1. Use an opaque projector to trace the lettering and the figures in the bulletin board illustration (page 137) on the background paper. Color appropriately.
2. Attach the library book card pockets to the board.
3. Cut and mark the brown posterboard pieces using the following surfboard pattern.

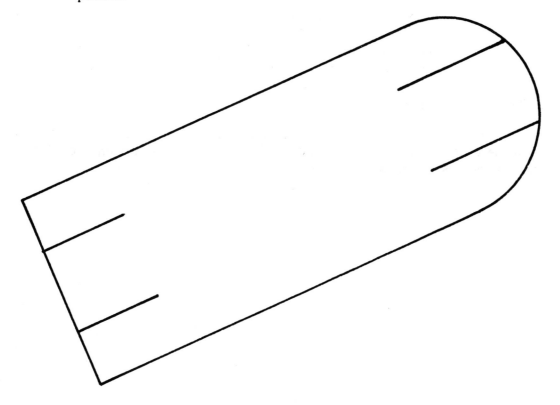

4. Print each of the following on a different surfboard.

> Card catalog, 135-136
> Cinquain poetry, 115
> Classifying, 56-58, 61
> Colon
> > in business letters, 216-217
> > in play directions, 26
>
> Comma
> > after an introductory word, 82
> > after closing of a letter, 210
>
> Commands or requests, 14, 29, 62
> Communicating, 53-54

5. Mark and attach the large envelope to the bulletin board. Place the surfboards in this envelope.

6. Fold the blue construction paper and mark the cover "Answer Key" as shown in the illustration. Copy the following on the inside and attach to the board.

> Card catalog, 135-136
> Cinquain poetry, 115
> Classifying, 56-58, 61
> Colon
> > in business letters, 216-217
> > in play directions, 26
>
> Comma
> > after an introductory word, 82
> > after closing of a letter, 210
>
> Commands or requests, 14, 29, 62
> Communicating, 53-54

Bulletin Board Activity:

This learning board may be used with children in the intermediate grades. Children are to place the surfboards in the order in which they would be found in an index. They may use the Answer Key when finished.

Bulletin Board Activities

SEE HOW HIGH YOU CAN FLY THE KITE

Skill Reinforced:

atlas usage

Materials Needed:

kite
blue background paper
felt-tipped pens (various colors)
construction paper (various colors)
white paper
scissors
stapler

Construction Directions:

1. Assemble the kite and attach it to the bulletin board.
2. Cut and mark the white paper using the cloud pattern in the bulletin board illustration on page 140. Attach this to the board.
3. Cut and mark a yellow sheet of construction paper using the butterfly pattern in the illustration. Attach this to the board.
4. Use an opaque projector to trace the lettering, the hand, the kite tail and string on the background paper.
5. Fold and cut the construction paper sheets as shown here to make the small kites.

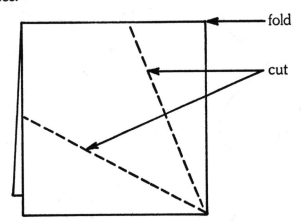

Bulletin Board Activities

6. Print each of the following sentences on the outside of a different kite. Print the corresponding YES or NO on the inside of each folded kite. Attach these to the board as shown in the illustration.

        Would you find a map of the U.S. in an atlas? (YES)
        Would you find the population of Germany in an atlas? (YES)
        Would an atlas give the rivers in Spain? (YES)
        Would you find your school telephone number in an atlas? (NO)
        Would you find a history of the U.S. in an atlas? (NO)
        Would an atlas show the ocean's currents? (YES)
        Would an atlas show the street map of your city? (NO)
        Would an atlas show the altitude levels in Africa? (YES)

Bulletin Board Activity:

This learning board is for children in the intermediate grades. Children read the information on each small kite and determine whether or not it could be found in an atlas. They may lift up the kites for the self-check.

Bulletin Board Activities

CAN YOU PICTURE THIS?

Skill Reinforced:

encyclopedia usage

Materials Needed:

white background paper
felt-tipped pens (various colors)
brown construction paper
white paper
stapler
glue

Construction Directions:

1. Use an opaque projector to trace the lettering and the giraffe figure in the bulletin board illustration (page 142) on the background paper. Color the giraffe appropriately.
2. Fold the brown construction paper and glue the white sheets on the front of each as shown here.

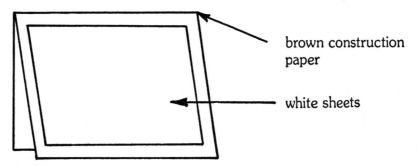

3. Print each of the following on the front of a different construction paper frame. Print the corresponding YES or NO under the flap.

   Facts about horses. (YES)
   Information about Woodrow Wilson. (YES)
   The size of Canada. (YES)
   The current rainfall in your home town. (NO)
   The telephone number of the White House. (NO)
   How many canoes are on the Indian River. (NO)

4. Attach these construction paper frames as shown in the illustration.

Bulletin Board Activity:

This learning board may be used with children in the intermediate grades. Children are to read the information on each frame, decide whether or not they would find it in an encyclopedia, and then lift the frame for the self-check.

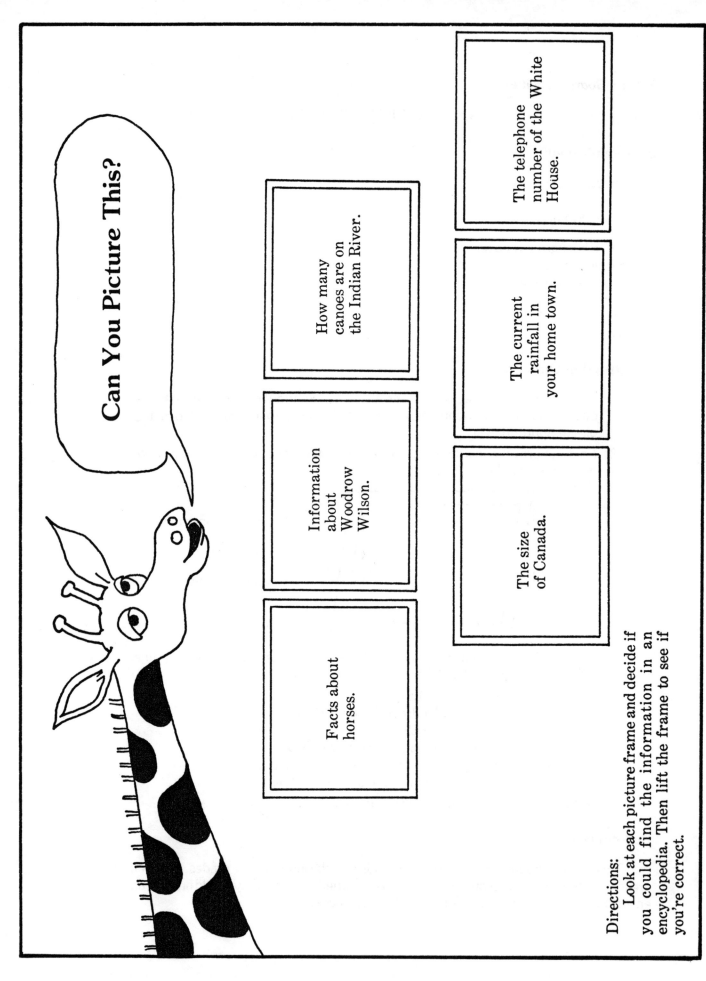

Bulletin Board Activities

QUACKER QUESTIONS

Skill Reinforced:

table of contents usage

Materials Needed:

green background paper
paper—blue, white, and yellow
felt-tipped pens (various colors)
blue construction paper
scissors
stapler
straight pins
legal size envelope
white posterboard

Construction Directions:

1. Use an opaque projector and trace the lettering in the bulletin board illustration on page 145 on the background paper.
2. Cut the blue paper into the pond shape as shown in the illustration. Cut the slits and mark the waves for the insertion of swan and fish.
3. Cut and mark the white paper using the swan shape and the yellow paper using the fish shape in the illustration.
4. Insert the fish and swan through the slits in the blue paper and attach it to the board.
5. Place the straight pins on the board and copy the chapter titles under each as in the illustration.
6. Cut and mark the white posterboard using the duck pattern shown here. You will need five ducks.

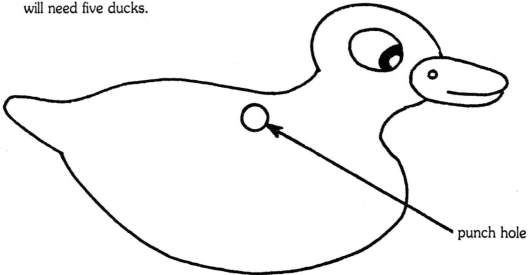

punch hole

7. Print each of the following questions on a different duck.

> Who were the early explorers who discovered America?
> The Puritans settled in what colonies?
> What caused the colonists to fight for independence?
> How many people lived in our new nation?
> When did the Louisiana Purchase take place?

8. Attach the large envelope to the board and place the ducks in it.
9. Fold the blue construction paper and mark the cover "Answer Key" as shown in the illustration.
10. Copy the following on the inside of the Answer Key and attach it to the board.

> Who were the early explorers who discovered America? in "Finding a New World"
> The Puritans settled in what colonies? in "The Thirteen Colonies"
> What caused the colonists to fight for independence? in "The Movement for Liberty"
> How many people lived in our new nation? in "Making a New Government"
> When did the Louisiana Purchase take place? in "Our Country Expands"

Bulletin Board Activity:

This learning board may be used by children in the intermediate grades. The children are to match the questions on the ducks to the chapter titles in which the answers would most likely be found. They may use the Answer Key when they finish.

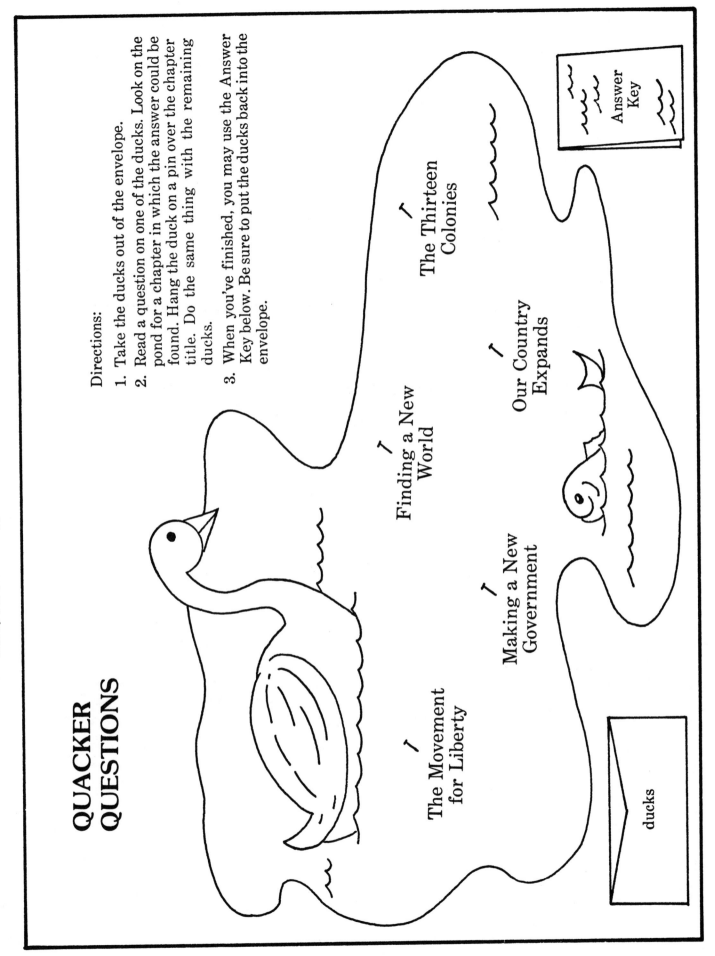

A "MONSTEROUS" VOCABULARY

Skill Reinforced:

dictionary skills

Materials Needed:

gray background paper
black felt-tipped pen

Construction Directions:

Use an opaque projector to trace the lettering and the figure in the bulletin board illustration (page 147) on the background paper.

Bulletin Board Activity:

This learning board may be used by children in the intermediate grades. The children are to look up the "monsterous" words in the dictionary.

A "Monsterous" Vocabulary

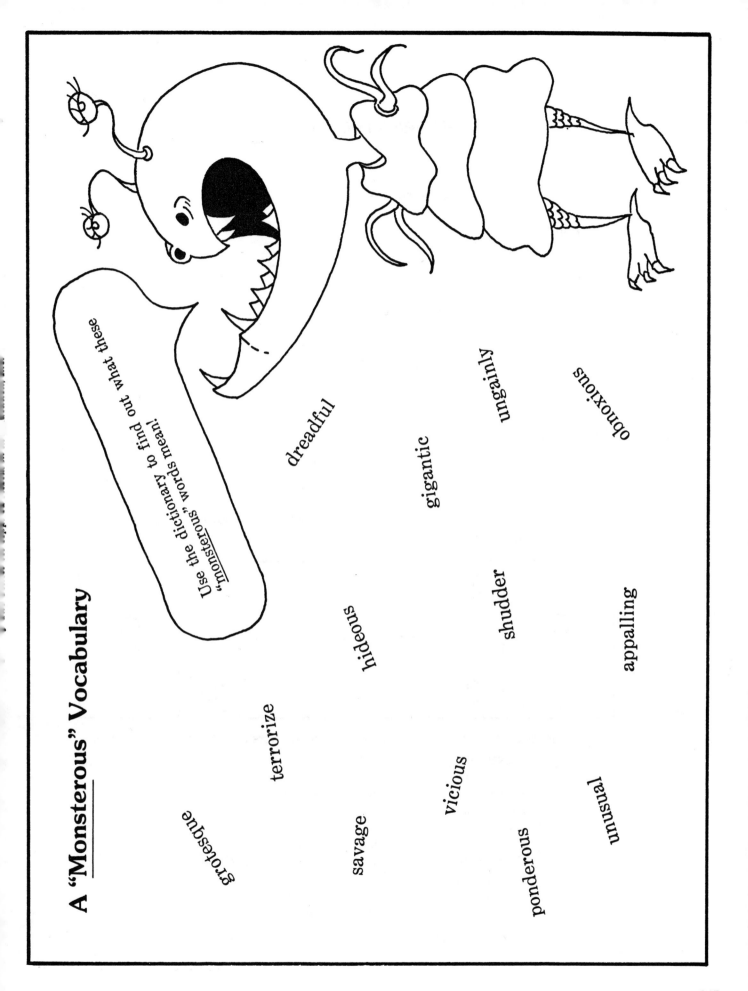

Use the dictionary to find out what these "monsterous" words mean!

grotesque
terrorize
dreadful
savage
hideous
gigantic
vicious
shudder
ungainly
ponderous
unusual
appalling
obnoxious

Bulletin Board Activities

WHERE'S THE BOOK?

Skill Reinforced:

location of fiction books on shelves

Materials Needed:

white background paper
library book card pockets
legal size envelope
felt-tipped pens (various colors)
posterboard of various colors
large laundry detergent box
construction paper—white and green
stapler
scissors

Construction Directions:

1. Use an opaque projector to trace the lettering and the shelf in the bulletin board illustration on page 150 onto the background paper. Color the letters yellow and the shelf brown.
2. Attach ten library book card pockets to the board as shown in the illustration.
3. Cut and mark the posterboard as shown here.

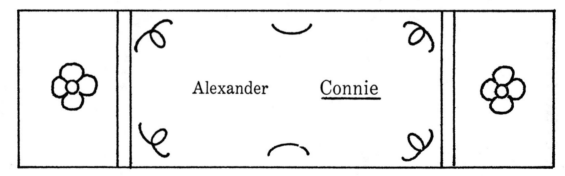

4. Print each of the following book titles and authors on a different book spine.

Alexander	*Connie*
Alexander	*To Live a Lie*
Angell	*Ronnie and Rosey*
Armstrong	*Sounder*
Banks	*My Darling Villain*
Bartch	*Good Old Ernie*
Bethancourt	*The Dog Days of Arthur Cane*
Bethancourt	*The Mortal Instruments*
Bethancourt	*Tune In Yesterday*
Blue	*A Month of Sundays*

Bulletin Board Activities

5. Fold the green construction paper and mark the "Answer Key" cover as shown in the illustration.
6. Copy the author/title list, in number 4, on the inside of the Answer Key and attach it to the board.
7. Mark and attach the envelope to the board and place the book spines in it.
8. Cover the detergent box with green and white construction paper so that it looks like a book, as shown in the illustration. Print the directions on it and attach it to the board.

Bulletin Board Activity:

This learning board may be used by children in the intermediate grades. They are to place the book spines in the pockets as they would expect to find them on the book shelves. When they are finished they may use the Answer Key.

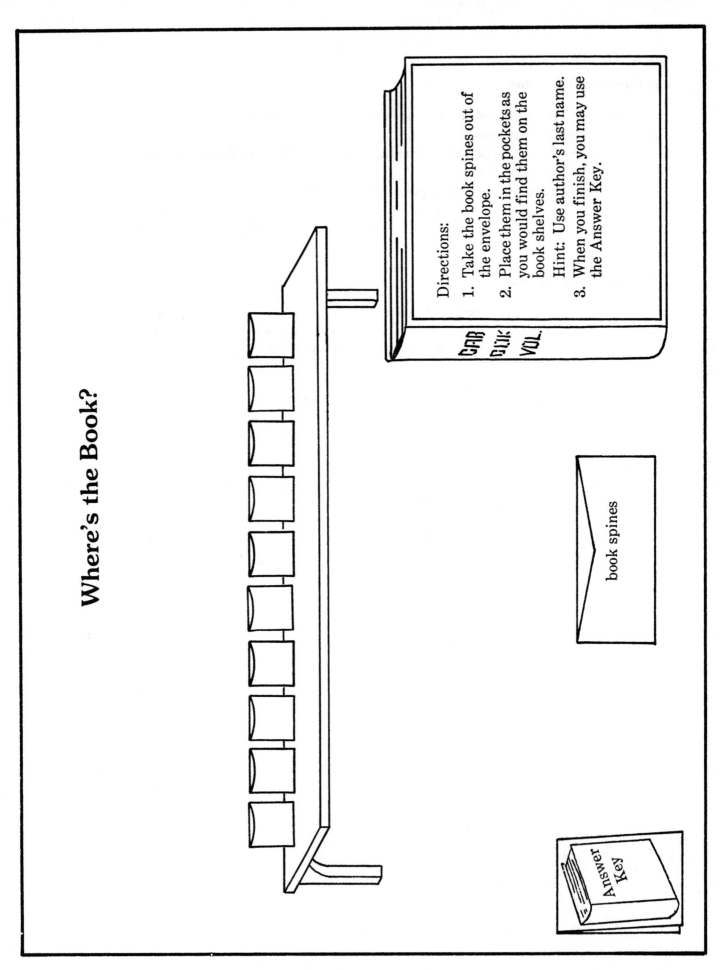

IV

Puzzle Pages

The puzzle pages in this section may be duplicated and used directly with students to reinforce a variety of library skills. While most of the puzzles are self-correcting, a key with answers to all of the puzzle activities is provided at the end of the section, pages 203-204.

Since children normally need a great deal of reinforcement when learning these skills, several different activity sheets are offered for each one. The activities are sequenced in order of difficulty, from primary through the high intermediate levels.

> **SUGGESTION:** A fine way to improve library skills *and* develop good public relations is to duplicate copies of appropriate puzzles and give them to teachers during Library Week, Children's Book Week, or just any time! Put the puzzles in a manila envelope or file folder and attach a copy of page 201 or 202 to the cover.

Following is a complete list of the puzzle activities, the library skill each one reinforces, and appropriate grade levels for use.

Puzzle Sheet	Library Skill	Grade Level
Shipshape	alphabetization	primary
A Table of What?	table of contents	primary
Stairway to the Moon	alphabetization	primary
Dave's Birthday	alphabetization	high primary
The Balloon That Got Away!	index usage	high primary
How Do You Know?	index usage	high primary
Arrange the Books	location of fiction books on shelves	high primary/ low intermediate
Take a Train Ride	guide word usage	high primary/ low intermediate

Puzzle Pages

Puzzle Sheet	Library Skill	Grade Level
Which Drawer?	card catalog usage	high primary/low intermediate
Let's Take a Trip!	index usage	high primary/low intermediate
Ski Jumping	guide word usage	high primary/low intermediate
What Country Are We In?	location of fiction books on shelves	high primary/low intermediate
Follow the Rainbow	location of fiction books on shelves	high primary/low intermediate
My Favorite!	guide word usage	high primary/intermediate
Oh No!	distinguishing fiction from nonfiction	high primary/intermediate
Crossing Death Valley	distinguishing fiction from nonfiction	high primary/intermediate
Symbols of America	dictionary skills	high primary/intermediate
What a Score!	table of contents usage	high primary/intermediate
An Artist	Dewey decimal classification	high primary/intermediate
Very Berry	Dewey decimal classification	high primary/intermediate
Be a Sport!	alphabetization	high primary/intermediate
Oh Gosh!	card catalog usage	high primary/intermediate
Suppose You Knew...	card catalog usage	high primary/intermediate
Presidents Puzzle	alphabetization	high primary/intermediate
Dogs... Dogs... Dogs!	guide word usage	intermediate
Guide Word Puzzle	guide word usage	intermediate
Tree Mania!	alphabetization	intermediate
High-Rise Apartments!	alphabetization	intermediate
A Visit to Their Grandparents	encyclopedia usage	intermediate
Buzz Off!	table of contents usage	intermediate
The Surprise!	encyclopedia usage	intermediate
Great Animals of the Past	alphabetization	intermediate
Index Information	index usage	intermediate
Look It Up!	index usage	intermediate

Puzzle Pages

Puzzle Sheet	Library Skill	Grade Level
Deep in the Ocean	atlas usage	intermediate
Walk Through the Forest	encyclopedia usage	intermediate
Colorful Contents	table of contents usage	intermediate
The High Jump	atlas usage	intermediate
Help for Jack!	encyclopedia usage	intermediate
It's Ancient History	table of contents usage	intermediate
Who Let in the Dog?	Dewey decimal classification	high intermediate
Follow the Flock!	Dewey decimal classification	high intermediate
The Mystery at Skull Mountain	Dewey decimal classification	high intermediate
In Chicago!	Dewey decimal classification	high intermediate
Word Search Puzzle	general library knowledge	high intermediate

Puzzle Pages

Shipshape

The first puzzle, on page 156, reinforces alphabetization skills and is designed for children in the primary grades. The children are to cut apart the strips on the broken lines and then place the strips in alphabetical order.

This puzzle sheet is self-correcting. A picture of a ship will be formed if the correct alphabetical order is followed.

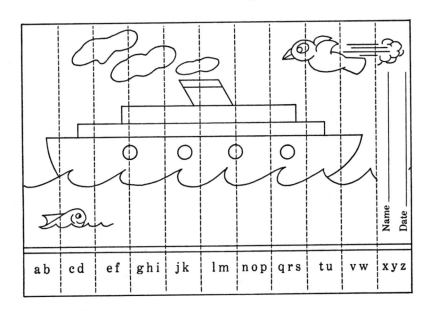

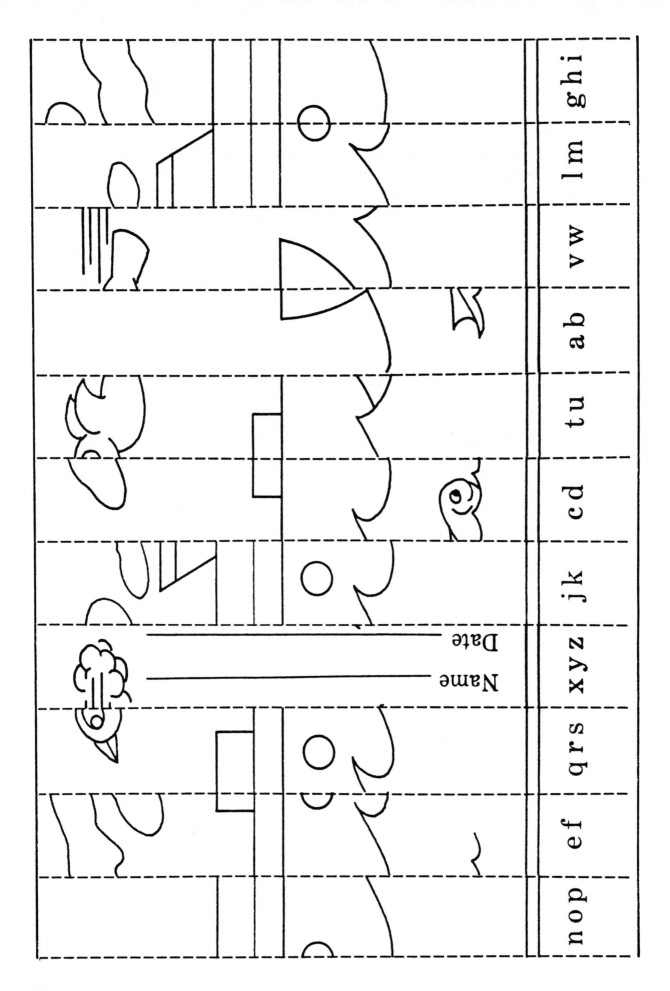

A Table of What?

Name _____

Date _____

Here is a table of contents. You are to look through it and then answer the questions.

```
TABLE OF CONTENTS
1  Friends .................   6
2  Staying Safe ...........  22
3  Our Senses .............  38
4  What Food Does .........  54
5  How We Grow ............  68
6  Clean and Healthy ......  84
7  What You Wear ..........  96
8  Stand Up Straight ...... 110
9  Families ............... 124
```

1. On what page does the chapter "How We Grow" begin? _____

2. How many chapters are in this book? _____

3. On what page does the seventh chapter begin? _____

4. What is the title of chapter two? _____

5. In which chapter would you look for information about food? _____

6. If you wanted to know more about your eyes, in which chapter would you look? _____

7. In which chapter would you look for advice about getting along with your brother or sister? _____

8. In which chapter would you look if you had to answer this question. "How many permanent teeth will you have by the time you are grown?" _____

Name _____

Date _____

Stairway to the Moon

Below is a stairway to the moon. You are to place the words in the star in the correct alphabetical order beginning at the top of the steps. Be sure to circle the letters circled in the star. If you are correct, the circled letters will spell the name of one of our planets.

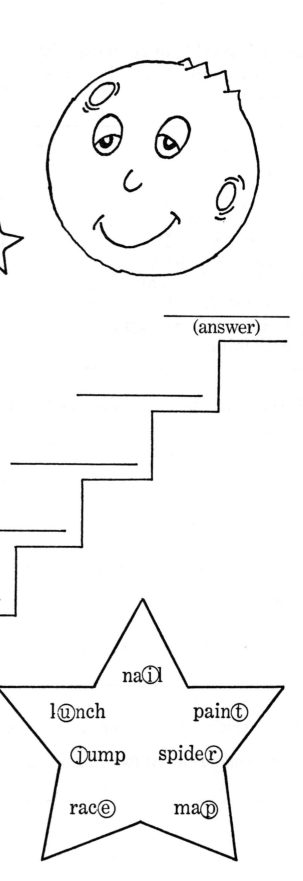

158

Name _____

Date _____

Dave's Birthday

Happy Birthday

Dave is having a birthday party tomorrow. Do you want to go? Before you can go you must do something. You must figure out how old Dave is! Don't guess yet! Below is a puzzle that will help you.

Look at the words in the package. These words are not in alphabetical order. You are to put them in alphabetical order by writing them in the blanks provided. Now copy the circled letters in the spaces at the bottom of this sheet. If you are correct, the circled letters will spell how old Dave will be tomorrow on his birthday. Have fun at the party!

_____
_____
_____
_____
_____
_____
_____
_____
_____
_____
_____
_____

eas(y)

gre(a)t

beg(i)n

dang(e)r

j(o)y

lea(d)

a(n)swer

kil(l)

increa(s)e

concer(n)

fr(e)e

ha(r)m

___ ___ ___ ___ ___ ___ ___ ___ ___ ___ ___ ___

The Balloon That Got Away!

"Oh no!" cried Henry. He had been holding his little sister's balloon when it slipped from his hand. He watched it float high into the sky, well beyond the clouds. Fortunately, he had enough money to buy her another. If you work the following puzzle, you can find out how old Henry's little sister is. Simply write the words, in the word box, on the spaces in the balloon's path. They must be in the order in which you would find them in an index. Be sure to circle the letters that are circled in the word box. If you are correct, the circled letters will spell the age of Henry's sister.

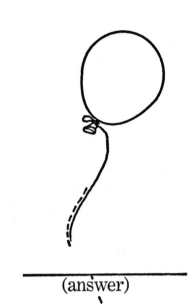

(answer)

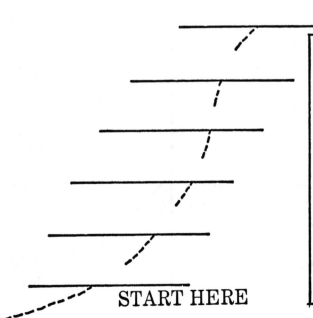

START HERE

WORD BOX
G(r)eat Britain, 49
Greenland curr(e)nt, 32
H(e)lsinki, 146
Gibral(t)ar, 31
Heyerd(a)hl, Thor, 105
Hud(s)on's Bay, 33
Hitle(r), Adolf, 49, 51
G(y)mnastics, 56
Gr(e)enland, 43
Got(h)s, 88

How Do You Know?

Name _____

Date _____

```
Accidents
    causes of, 22-26
    in the home, 22-26
    on the street, 28-31
    prevention of, 22-23
Activities, 21, 37, 53, 67, 82, 95,
    109, 123, 137
Bones, 118-119
Brain, 40-41, 44, 46, 118
Burns, 25, 27
Cells, 58, 71
Cereals, 57
Cleanliness
    baths, 84-87
    keeping clothes clean, 102-104
Clothing
    care of, 102-105
    that fits you, 100-101
    and the weather, 96-99
Colds, 47-48
Courtesy
    being a good guest, 130-131
    being thoughtful of others, 7-10,
        76-79, 130-133
    making introductions, 8
Dentist, 75
Digestion, 62-63
Doctor, 91
Ears, 41, 44-45
Exercise
    and growth, 71
    and posture, 119, 120-121
    and strength, 19, 51, 65, 92, 107,
        117, 119, 120, 135
Eyes, 38, 39, 41, 42-43
Families
    being thoughtful, 76-79, 130-133
    doing your share of work, 78, 133, 138
    getting along with brothers and
        sisters, 124-129
    obeying parents, 78, 130, 131, 132
    sharing fun, 88-89, 133
```

How do you know where to look for something in a book? Well, you could use the index. Here is an index. You are to look through it and then answer the questions.

1. On which pages would you look in order to find information about burns? _____

2. On which pages would you find information about street accidents? _____

3. You should go to the dentist twice a year. On what page would you find information about this?

   _____

4. Which topic listed in this index seems to be referred to most in this book? _____

   _____

5. On what pages would you look to find information about being courteous when you visit someone?

   _____

Arrange the Books

Name _____

Date _____

Let's see how good you are at arranging fiction books in the library. Below is a list of books along with their authors. You are to put them in the same order as you would find the books if they were in a library. That is, according to the author's last name. Write them, in order, on the spaces provided. Be sure to circle the letters that are circled in the list. When you are finished, copy the circled letters in the blanks provided at the bottom of this sheet. If you are correct, the circled letters will spell how well you did!

White Snow, Bright Snow by Alvin Tre(s)selt
Bluebe(r)ries for Sal by Robert McCloskey
Tales of a Fou(r)th Grade Nothing by Judy Blume
Soup for Presi(d)ent by Robert Peck
Ramona the Pest by Beverl(y) Cleary
Ramon(a) the Brave by Beverly Cleary
Isabelle the I(t)ch by Constance Greene
Onc(e) a Mouse by Marcia Brown
Ramona and Her Mother by Beverl(l)y Cleary
Tim(e) of Wonder by Robert McCloskey
Ramona and Her Father by Beverl(l)y Cleary
Burt Dow, D(e)ep Water Man by Robert McCloskey
(M)ake Way for Ducklings by Robert McCloskey
Sam, Ba(n)gs and Moonshine by Evaline Ness
The Beaver P(o)nd by Alvin Tresselt
S(u)n Up by Alvin Tresselt

1. _____
2. _____
3. _____
4. _____
5. _____
6. _____
7. _____
8. _____
9. _____
10. _____
11. _____
12. _____
13. _____
14. _____
15. _____
16. _____

___ ___ ___ ___ ___ ___ ___ ___ ___ ___ ___ ___ ___ ___ ___ ___

Take a Train Ride

Name _____

Date _____

ma(h)ogany   mar(g)in
m(a)nage   ma(c)hine
maro(o)n   malar(i)a
malpracti(c)e

This train is going to a city that you might like to visit. What city? Well, there's a way for you to find out. Follow the train track. When you come to the guide words, look in the caboose for the word that would fit on that page. Write this word in the appropriate space. Be sure to circle the letters in each word that are circled in the caboose. When you are finished, copy the circled letters in the spaces at the bottom of this sheet. If you are correct, these letters will spell the city to which the train is going.

market — marry
_____

manner — mark
_____

man — mane
_____

major — male
_____

mall — malt
_____

magic — mail
_____

mace — made
_____

START HERE

_ _ _ _ _ _ _

163

Which Drawer?

Name _____

Date _____

Here is a list of books. You are to decide the card catalog drawer in which you would find a card for that book. Write the letters on that drawer on the space next to the book below.

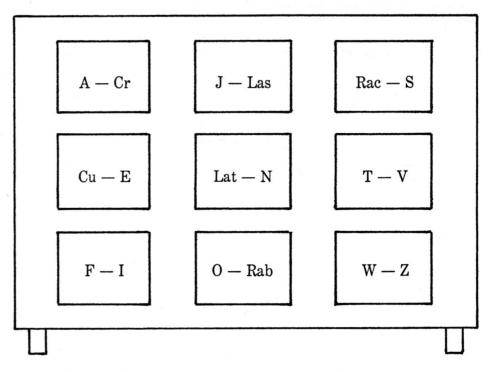

_____ 1. A book by Constance Greene.

_____ 2. A book on astronomy.

_____ 3. A book called Queen of Hearts.

_____ 4. A book by Scott O'Dell.

_____ 5. A book about sound.

_____ 6. A book of poetry.

_____ 7. A book by Carl Withers.

_____ 8. A book called Good Old Ernie.

_____ 9. A book by Marian R. Bartch.

_____ 10. A book about oceans.

_____ 11. A book about dogs.

_____ 12. A book called Nikki 108.

_____ 13. A book by S.E. Hinton.

_____ 14. A book about canoes.

_____ 15. A book called Sounder.

164

Let's Take a Trip!

Name _____

Date _____

The Bond family is taking a trip. Do you think you can guess where they are going? Well, there is a way for you to find out. Simply cut out the word boxes and place them in the order in which you would find them in an index, beginning at the car. If you are correct, the circled letters will spell where the Bond family is going!

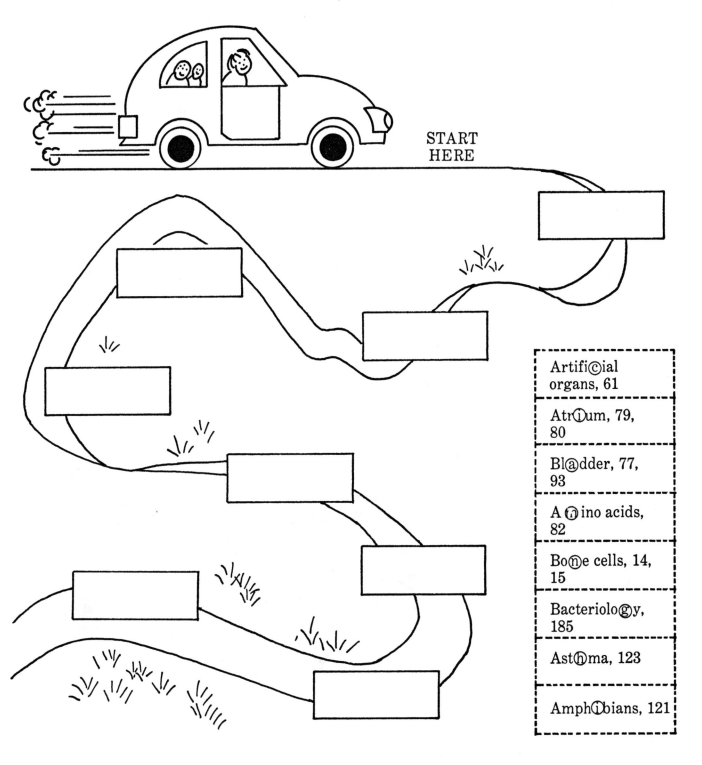

Artifi©ial organs, 61

Atrⓘum, 79, 80

Bl@dder, 77, 93

A Ⓝino acids, 82

Boⓝe cells, 14, 15

Bacteriolo⑨y, 185

Astⓗma, 123

Amphⓘbians, 121

Name _____

Date _____

Ski Jumping

How are you at ski jumping? Well, you can try it now. Begin at the top of the hill and "push off." When you come to the guide words, look in the cabin for the word that would fit on that page. Write this word in the appropriate space. Be sure to circle the letters that are circled in the words in the cabin. When you are finished, copy the circled letters in the spaces at the bottom of this sheet. If you are correct, these letters will spell a place where you could go ski jumping.

START HERE

_____ saber — sack

_____ sad — safe

_____ said — sale

_____ salt — same

_____ sample — sand

_____ sane — satin

_____ satisfy — save

_____ saw — scale

_____ score — section

_____ scalp — scope

sate(l)lite
sab(l)e   salut(e)
sc(i)ence   s(a)uce
sa(k)e
                  sam(p)ler
s(a)ddle   secon(d)   s(c)ab

_ _ _ _ _ _ _ _ _ _

166

Name _____

Date _____

What Country Are We In?

Below are two puzzles. In each puzzle is a list of fiction books. You are to place them in the order in which they would be found in a library. Do this by writing them in the spaces provided. Be sure to circle the letters that are circled in the lists. If you are correct, the circled letters in each puzzle will spell the name of a country.

Puzzle One:

The Saving of P.S. by Robbi(e) Branscum

Ellen (G)rae by Vera and Bill Cleaver

Where's (M)ark by Jacquie Hann

Johnny May by Ro(b)bie Branscum

(U)p Day, Down Day by Jacquie Hann

Grover by Vera and B(i)ll Cleaver

Three Buckets of Day(l)ight by Robbie Branscum

Puzzle Two:

(S)oup and Me by Robert Peck

Frog, Where Are Yo(u)? by Mercer Mayer

A Bi(l)lion for Boris by Mary Rodgers

Where the Sidewalk Ends by Shel S(i)lverstein

It's Not F(a)ir by Robyn Supraner

A Bo(y), a Dog and a Frog by Mercer Mayer

I Do Not Like It by I(v)an Sherman

Fre(a)ky Friday by Mary Rodgers

One Fro(g) Too Many by Mercer Mayer

S(o)up by Robert Peck

_____
_____
_____
_____
_____
_____
_____

_____
_____
_____
_____
_____
_____
_____
_____
_____
_____

© 1981 by The Center for Applied Research in Education, Inc.

Follow the Rainbow

Name _____

Date _____

See if you can follow the rainbow to where the pot-of-gold is located. Simply look at the fiction books in the pot-of-gold and place them on the rainbow in the same order in which you would find them in a library. Be sure to circle the letters that are circled in the pot. If you are correct, the circled letters will spell the place where the pot-of-gold is hidden. Begin at the top of the rainbow and work down.

START HERE

(answer)

H(o)w to Lose Your Lunch Money by Florence White
Ira Sl(e)eps Over by Bernard Waber
Rosie and Michael by Judi(t)h Viorst
The (D)ogs' Present by Charlotte Zolotow
Deep in the Forest by Br(i)nton Turkle
I'll Fix A(n)thony by Judith Viorst
(S)omeday by Charlotte Zolotow
Mice on My Mind by Bernard (W)aber
But Names Will Never (H)urt Me by Bernard Waber
No B(o)dy Is Perfect by Bernard Waber

© 1981 by The Center for Applied Research in Education, Inc.

Name _____

Date _____

My Favorite!

"What's your favorite holiday?" asked Dave.
"Oh ... I think Christmas," answered Chris.
"Well, it's not mine!" said Dave.
"What is yours?" asked Chris.
"I'm not going to tell," replied Dave.
  Well, there is a way for you to find out Dave's favorite holiday. Below are guide words each followed by a list of three words. You are to decide which of the three list words would be found on the same page as the guide words. Write this word on the space next to the guide words. Be sure to circle the letters that are circled on this sheet on your choices. If you are correct, the circled letters will spell Dave's favorite holiday.

(1) obscure — obvious   _____
    o(b)serve
    occasio(n)
    oa(r)
(2) key — knock   _____
    knuckl(e)
    k(i)ck
    ketc(h)
(3) pepper — period   _____
    peri(s)h
    pe(o)ple
    pe(r)cept
(4) sale — same   _____
    sal(t)
    sai(l)
    sanctio(n)
(5) coffee — coin   _____
    co(h)ere
    col(d)
    colle(g)e
(6) race — radish   _____
    raccoo(n)
    ra(d)io
    raf(t)
(7) want — warm   _____
    wak(e)
    wa(d)dle
    w(a)r
(8) plastic — plea   _____
    pla(y)
    plea(d)
    pleas(e)

169

"Oh boy," thought Janice. "Now I'm going to get it!" Janice had gone into her older brother Ned's room to borrow a book and accidentally knocked over his bookshelf. Luckily for Janice, Ned was not home. "I better get these books back on the bookshelf," she thought as she began picking up books. Ned kept his books on two different shelves, one for fiction and the other for his nonfiction books. You can help Janice put the books on their proper shelves. Below is a list of some of Ned's books. You are to determine which books should be categorized as fiction. Put an F next to each of these books. When you are finished, copy the circled letters in the F books on the spaces provided at the bottom of this sheet. If you are correct, the letters will spell the name of the place where Ned is. Now hurry before Ned gets home!

IMPORTANT: Use the card catalog if you need to!

_____ Blub(b)er by Judy Blume
_____ Wh(a)leboat Raid by Peter Burchard
_____ Wha(t) Makes a Clock Tick? by Chester Johnson
_____ Fire in the (S)tone by Colin Thiele
_____ America's Ho(r)ses and Ponies by Irene Brady
_____ Soup and M(e) by Robert Peck
_____ (B)ecky's Horse by Winifred Madison
_____ The Other W(a)y Around by Judith Kerr
_____ Isabel(l)e the Itch by Constance Greene
_____ Chi(l)d of Fire by Scott O'Dell
_____ The P(u)eblo Indians by Richard Erdoes
_____ Football Talk fo(r) Beginners by Howard Liss
_____ Just the Be(g)inning by Betty Miles
_____ The Pinb(a)lls by Betsy Byars
_____ Bla(c)k American Leaders by Margaret Young
_____ Me and Ji(m) Luke by Robbie Branscum
_____ Sea She(l)ls of the World by R. Tucker Abbott
_____ Mr. Myst(e)rious and Company by Sid Fleishman

___ ___ ___ ___ ___ ___ ___   ___ ___ ___ ___

170

Crossing Death Valley

Name _____

Date _____

Help the old prospector cross Death Valley. As you follow his path you must stop at each cactus you come to. Under each cactus is the title of a book. If you think the book would be found in the nonfiction section of your library you should copy down the circled letter in the title on the spaces at the bottom of this sheet. If you are correct, the circled letters will spell how long it took the old prospector to cross Death Valley.

IMPORTANT: Use the card catalog if you need to!

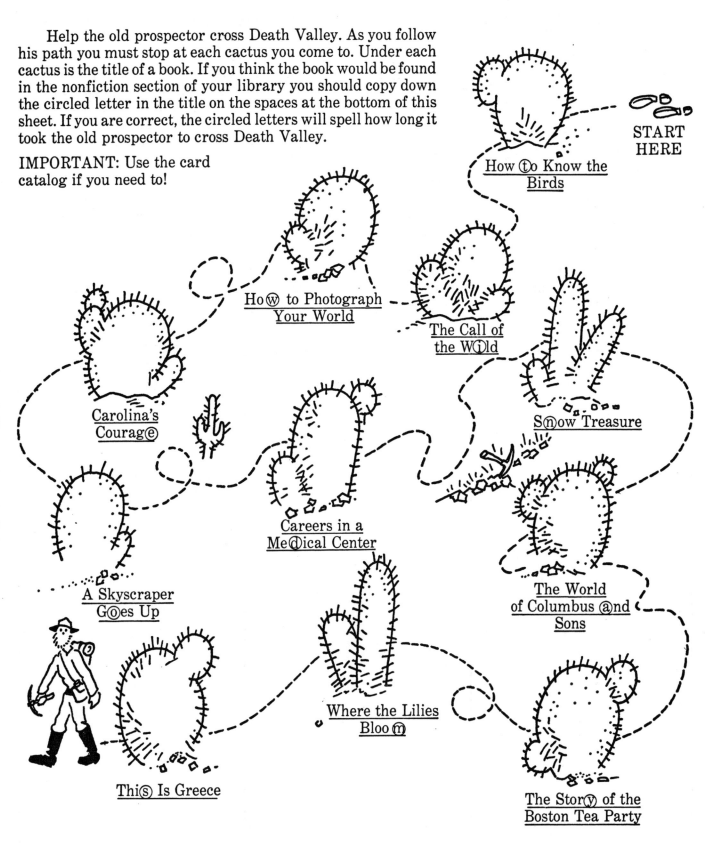

START HERE

How (t)o Know the Birds

Ho(w) to Photograph Your World

The Call of the W(i)ld

Carolina's Courag(e)

S(n)ow Treasure

Careers in a Me(d)ical Center

A Skyscraper G(o)es Up

The World of Columbus (a)nd Sons

Where the Lilies Bloo(m)

Thi(s) Is Greece

The Stor(y) of the Boston Tea Party

___ ___ ___ ___ ___ ___ ___ ___

171

Symbols of America

Name _____

Date _____

Below is a list of words. You are to decide in which section of a dictionary (front, middle or back) each word would be found. Write each word under the appropriate heading on this sheet. Be sure to circle the letters that are circled in the list. If you are correct, the circled letters under each heading will spell a special symbol of our country.

1. bru(s)h
2. moth(b)all
3. collec(t)
4. ev(a)de
5. kn(a)p
6. watchf(u)l
7. reputatio(n)
8. dolla(r)
9. bli(s)ter
10. fami(l)y
11. pai(d)
12. el(a)stic
13. brow(n)
14. g(e)nius
15. ide(a)l
16. ro(c)k
17. quil(l)
18. crow(d)
19. a(s)k
20. dis(t)ance
21. se(e)d
22. tru(s)t
23. exp(r)ess
24. br(i)ng
25. mira(g)e
26. oi(l)
27. a(p)ple
28. dang(e)rous
29. str(a)w
30. vita(m)in
31. num(e)ral
32. di(s)h

FRONT (a-e)	MIDDLE (f-p)	BACK (q-z)

Name _____

Date _____

What a Score!

The Arlington Red Devils went into the game as underdogs ... but they were ready! By halftime, they were even with the Arcadia Indians. The score stood 12 to 12. The fans went wild when the teams came back onto the field. The game was exciting especially for the Red Devils since they won the game. The final score was _____ to 19. If you want to know the final score for the Red Devils, simply work the following puzzle. You are to read each question in the goal post, and decide in which chapter the answer would be found. Write the circled letter in the questions next to the appropriate chapter titles. If you are correct, the circled letters will spell the Red Devils' final score.

_____ Kinds of Birds

_____ What Birds Eat

_____ Importance of Birds

_____ Home Life of Birds

_____ The Bodies of Birds

_____ How Birds Fly

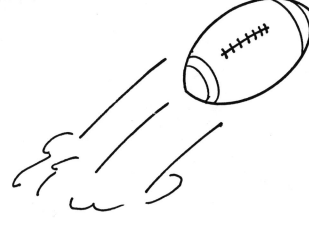

What kinds of seeds should you put out during the (w)inter?
How do birds h(e)lp the farmer?
How do feathers help birds fl(y)?
What (t)ypes of birds live in the tropics?
What is the body (t)emperature of birds?
Why do more ki(n)ds of birds live on land than on water?

© 1981 by The Center for Applied Research in Education, Inc.

An Artist

"It is!" said Joe.
"It is not!" said Sam.
"Well, I think it is!"
"A lot you know!"
"What on earth is this argument about?" asked the boys' father. The brothers are with their father at the city's Art Museum and are arguing about one of the paintings. Joe thinks he knows who the artist is but Sam disagrees. You can solve the argument! Below is a list of nonfiction books. You are to read through the list and place those which you think you'd find in The Arts (700-799) section of your library in the spaces next to this list. Be sure to circle the letters that are circled in the list. If you're correct, the circled letters will spell the name of the artist the boys are arguing over.

Looking at Scul(p)ture
Daniel Boon(e)
C(u)ba
All About the Weathe(r)
Art of Colon(i)al America
Dis(c)overing Pottery
America's Be(g)innings
The U(n)iverse
How to M(a)ke Things Out of Paper
Custer's Last Stan(d)
A Bird Is Bor(n)
American Folk Song(s)
Grea(t) Religions
Com(e)ts
Song(s) of the Chippewa
Story of the Boston Tea Part(y)
Dis(c)overing Design

Very Berry

Name _____

Date _____

Nonfiction books are factual, informational types of material. These are arranged by a code number that groups the books in classes. Below is a list of nonfiction books. You are to place them in the appropriate columns according to their category. Be sure to circle the letters that are circled on this sheet. If you are correct, the circled letters in each column will spell a kind of fruit.

500-599 Pure Science   900-999 History

_____   Pl(a)nts Without Leaves   _____

_____   Colonial Ameri(c)a   _____

_____   (H)ow Our First Settlers Survived   _____

_____   Ex(p)loring the Stars   _____

_____   Th(e) Civil War   _____

_____   Discove(r)ing the New World   _____

Kitchen Ex(p)eriments

Al(l) about the Sea

First Book of Flow(e)rs

Ancient G(r)eece

Last Centur(y) Europe

Hibernating Animal(s)

© 1981 by The Center for Applied Research in Education, Inc.

175

Name _____

Date _____

Below is a list of words. Look at the first row of words. Find the word that would come before the underlined word in a dictionary. Write this word in the space next to the underlined word. Be sure to circle the letters that are circled on this sheet. If you are correct, the circled letters will spell the name of a sport.

_____ jade   ja(m), jacke(t), janito(r)

_____ imitation   imitat(e), imm(a)ture, immed(i)ate

_____ hire   hi(s), histo(r)y, hi(n)ge

_____ golf   golde(n), (g)one, goo(d)

_____ radish   rad(i)o, r(a)dium, radi(u)s

_____ thaw   (t)he, theate(r), thank(s)

If you're brave, try this brain-twister! The circled letters will spell the name of another sport if you're correct.

_____ hockey   hol(d), ho(b)by, (h)ole

_____ mortgage   mort(a)l, m(o)st, mot(i)ve

_____ pool   po(p)corn, po(r)k, pon(d)

_____ fence   fe(m)ale, fer(n), fer(t)ile

_____ alcove   alga(e), album(i)n, (a)live

_____ brand   bra(n)ch, bras(s), brea(k)

_____ recourse   re(c)ruit, (r)ecreate, recoun(t)

_____ sport   spo(u)se, spr(e)ad, spo(o)n

_____ lenient   len(s), le(n)gth, leopa(r)d

176

"Oh gosh!" complained Bill to himself, "I never will find all these books!"

Bill had a list of books to look up in the card catalog for an English assignment. The problem was that it was taking longer than he thought it would. He was planning to go to a movie with his friend Sam but it looked as if he might not be able to make it. You can help Bill meet his friend at the movie theater. Simply copy the book titles from his paper on the correct order of the card catalog drawers in which they would be found. Be sure to circle the letters circled on his paper. When you are finished, copy the circled letters on the blanks at the bottom of this sheet. If you are correct, they will spell the movie Bill and Sam are planning to see.

Remember ... if a title begins with <u>a</u>, <u>an</u> or <u>the</u>, you look for it in the card catalog under the second word!

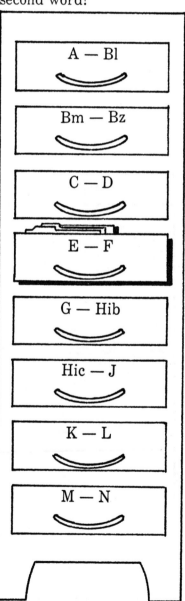

<u>A Book for ⓉOny</u>
<u>The Goof That Ⓦon the Pennant</u>
<u>A Little BⓇeathing Room</u>
<u>AbⓈolute Zero</u>
<u>The Edge of Next YeaⓇ</u>
<u>I'm Deborⓐh Sampson</u>
<u>My Brother Sam IⓈ Dead</u>
<u>The Cⓐbin Faced West</u>

_____
_____
_____
_____
_____
_____
_____
_____

__ __ __   __ __ __ __

Name _____

Date _____

Suppose You Knew...

Suppose you were looking for a book and only knew... well, let's say you knew very little about the book. Maybe you knew only what the book was about, the author or just the title. How would you go about finding the book? Where would you look in the card catalog? Well, this is what you're to do here. Below is a list of items. You are to determine whether you would look for the subject card, author card or title card. Copy them in the appropriate lists. Be sure to circle the letters that are circled in the list. If you are correct, the circled letters in each list will spell a kind of animal.

<u>The Dangerou(s) Game</u>
<u>C(h)arlotte's Web</u>
Janet (H)ickman
sta(r)s
(o)cean

base(b)all
Jer(o)me Brooks
Bette G(r)een
<u>Th(e) King's Fifth</u>
Katherine Pater(s)on

b(i)rds
<u>Crossing the Lin(e)</u>
<u>My Brother's (P)lace</u>
Scott O'D(e)ll
heari(n)g

AUTHOR	TITLE	SUBJECT

178

Presidents Puzzle

Name _____

Date _____

Below is a "Presidents Puzzle." In order to spell a president's name you must look at each row of words, choose the word that would come first in your dictionary and write it in the space next to that row of words. Be sure to circle the letters that are circled on this sheet. If you are correct, the circled letters will spell the name of one of our presidents.

_____ skim(p) (s)ling s(m)ear

_____ forma(l) f(o)rm for(m)ality

_____ dema(n)d defau(l)t degrad(e)

_____ (c)log cloc(k) clo(d)

If you're brave, try this next Presidents Puzzle!

_____ accomp(l)ished accomplis(h) acco(r)d

_____ (a)lmond alm(o)st alof(t)

_____ bankrup(t) bankin(g) banke(r)

_____ calibe(r) calic(o) calibrat(e)

_____ gramm(a)r gra(i)n gra(n)d

_____ interesti(n)g interf(e)re intere(s)t

_____ mediu(m) meditati(o)n m(e)dley

_____ st(r)engthen s(t)renuous stre(n)gth

179

Dogs ... Dogs ... Dogs!

Name _____

Date _____

Below is a guide word puzzle. That is, a pair of guide words followed by a list of words. You are to look through the list of words and write down those that would be found on the same page as the guide words. Be sure to circle the letters that are circled in the list. If you are correct, the circled letters will spell a kind of dog.

baby — banquet
   baboo(n)
   back(p)ack
   backwo(o)ds
   b(a)bble
   balc(o)ny
   bal(d)
   (b)ay
   ba(t)h
   bal(l)oon
   barbe(r)
   bann(e)r

Now try this next guide word puzzle.

salmon — sank
   sa(f)ety
   sa(l)e
   san(c)tify
   sal(o)n
   (s)ail
   sa(l)t
   sa(l)vage
   sac(k)
   sa(d)dle
   sacre(d)
   san(i)ty
   sa(f)e
   san(e)

Guide Word Puzzle

Name _____

Date _____

Find the word in each sentence that alphabetically fits between the guide words above that particular sentence. Write it in the space next to the guide words. If you are correct, the first letter of the words you write in the spaces will spell how well you did. Good Luck!

(1) valve — varnish _____
   I couldn't decide what kind of ice cream to have because they had such a large variety of flavors.

(2) erase — ethical _____
   What do you estimate the answer to be?

(3) race — rayon _____
   She made it to the house just before it started to rain.

(4) yacht — yell _____
   In what year did he have the mumps?

(5) gripe — growl _____
   The brown wolf dug a large hole in the ground.

(6) our — oven _____
   I explained the outline with the teacher.

(7) object — odd _____
   Yesterday I observed an elderly person jump across that creek.

(8) dishonor — displace _____
   Our dishwasher is not getting our glasses clean enough.

Tree Mania!

Name _____

Date _____

Look below at the sample list of three words. These words are not in alphabetical order. You are to put them in the correct order by writing them in the blanks next to the list. Be sure to circle the letter in each word that has been circled in the list. If you are correct, the circled letters will spell a kind of tree.

h(a)m _____
hand(k)erchief _____
hal(o) _____

How did you do? You should have spelled the word OAK. Now try the rest of the lists. Remember, each list will spell a type of tree if you're correct.

Puzzle One:

n(a)p _____

nationa(l) _____

nativ(e) _____

na(p)kin _____

na(m)e _____

Puzzle Two:

(c)age _____

cab(i)n _____

carbo(h)ydrate _____

ca(b)bage _____

cafete(r)ia _____

Puzzle Three:

tailo(r) _____

tambo(u)rine _____

targ(e)t _____

table(s)poon _____

tapio(c)a _____

tad(p)ole _____

Puzzle Four:

sab(o)tage _____

s(a)crifice _____

saf(e)ty _____

sac(r)ed _____

safe(g)uard _____

sacrosa(n)ct _____

High-Rise Apartments!

Sandy lives in the Pleasant View Apartment Building. She lives on the top floor. Can you guess which floor this is? Here is a way for you to find out!

The words in the small building next to Sandy's are all jumbled around. You are to put these in alphabetical order beginning with the blank at the top of the Pleasant View Apartment Building. Be sure to circle the letter that is circled in the jumbled words.

When you have finished, begin again at the top of the Apartment Building and write the circled letters in the blanks at the bottom of this sheet. If you are correct, these letters will spell the number of the floor on which Sandy lives.

amat(e)ur   amu(s)e   al(w)ays
ancho(v)y   al(t)ernate   ang(e)l
ambitio(n)   ambi(t)ious   amnest(y)
amus(e)d   a(n)ger

___ ___ ___ ___ ___ ___ ___   ___ ___ ___ ___

A Visit to Their Grandparents

Name _____

Date _____

"Look out the window, Bobby," said his sister Brenda.
"Oh gosh!" said Bobby. "Isn't it beautiful?"
"It sure is."
"The first thing I'm going to do is go swimming," said Bobby excitedly.
"Me too," echoed Brenda.

Brenda and Bobby are going to visit their grandparents for two weeks. Now where do you suppose their grandparents live? You can find out by working the following puzzle. Place the list of topics in the order in which you would find them in an encyclopedia index. Be sure to circle the letters that are circled in the list. If you are correct, the circled letters will spell where Brenda and Bobby's grandparents live.

_____	Tambo(u)rine
_____	Soci(e)ty of Tammany
_____	Tasmanian Devi(l)
_____	Taft-Ha(r)tley Act
_____	Tanza(n)ia
_____	Taxat(i)on
_____	T(a)nnic Acid
_____	Edwar(d) Taylor
_____	William Howard Taf(t)
_____	Un(i)versity of Tampa
_____	Tap (D)ancing
_____	Tagus Riv(e)r
_____	T'ang Dyna(s)ty
_____	Tanimbar Is(l)ands
_____	Tarif(f)
_____	Tasmanian W(o)lf
_____	T(a)iping Rebellion
_____	M(a)xwell Taylor
_____	Taming of the Sh(r)ew
_____	Tax Cou(r)t of the United States
_____	Tallaha(s)see

Name _____

Date _____

Buzz Off!

Our bee seems to be angry. It appears that he cannot find his favorite kind of flower. Work the following puzzle and find out what kind of flower that is! You are to read each question in the beehive, and decide in which chapter the answer would be found. Write the circled letter in each question next to the appropriate chapter. If you are correct, the circled letters will spell a kind of flower.

START HERE

The Importance of Plants ___

Kinds of Plants ___

Where Plants Live ___

Parts of Plants ___

How Plants Reproduce ___

How Plants Grow ___

How Plants Change ___

A Classification of the Plant Kingdom ___

Beehive questions:

- What is cross-pollinatio(n)?
- In what ways do yo(u) think plants have changed over the years?
- How do green plants make the(i)r own food?
- What is the purpose of the le(a)f?
- How do plants su(r)vive on the desert?
- About how many kinds of plants ar(e) there?
- Why are flowering plants called angiosper(m)s?
- What foods do plants (g)ive us?

185

The Surprise!

Name _____

Date _____

"Hi Dad!" hollered John.
"Hi, yourself!" yelled John's dad. "Come down here and see what I brought home."
John raced down the steps taking two at a time.
"It's outside," said his dad.
"Wow!" exclaimed John.

Now what do you suppose John's dad brought home? Well, work the following puzzle and find out. Simply place the list of topics in the order in which you would find them in an encyclopedia index. Be sure to circle the letters that are circled in the list. If you are correct, the circled letters will spell what John's dad brought home.

_____   Rock(y) Marciano

_____   Marasch(i)no Cherries

_____   Mare Is(l)and Naval Shipyard

_____   Maple Sug(a)r

_____   Battle of Mar(e)ngo

_____   Mar(c)us Island

_____   Maracai(b)o

_____   Gabriel Mar(c)el

By working the next puzzle you can find out what kind of a _____ John's dad brought home!

_____   Garbage Dis(p)osal

_____   James A. Garfi(e)ld

_____   Mohanda(s) Gandhi

_____   Galves(t)on

_____   Or(d)er of the Garter

_____   Gard(e)ning

_____   Gambi(e)r Islands

_____   Indira Ga(n)dhi

Name _____

Date _____

Great Animals of the Past

"Dinosaurs lived many years ago," read Greg. He was reading a report he had written to his class at school. "Most of these animals were very large in size. The largest meat-eating dinosaur was a _____."

"Oh no," thought Greg. "I forgot to look up that name." Quick! You can help Greg discover the name of this dinosaur by putting the following words in their correct alphabetical order. Be sure to circle the letters that are circled on this sheet. If you are correct, the circled letters will spell the name of this dinosaur.

_____ fal(s)e

_____ fai(n)t

_____ f(a)ctory

_____ facilit(y)

_____ fancie(r)

_____ f(a)lsify

_____ fanta(s)tic

_____ famo(u)s

_____ face(t)

_____ fancif(u)l

_____ Fahre(n)heit

_____ falc(o)n

_____ facto(r)

187

Name _____

Date _____

Index Information

You are to look through the following index and then answer the questions.

```
Sensory words, 105-109, 150
Sentence transforms, see Transforms
Sentences
    cause-and-effect, 175, 188, 262
    time-order, 177, 188, 262
Simile, 114-116, 121, 150
Slogans, 210-211, 217
Smear words, 209-210
Speaking
    group planning, 73-74, 84
    improvisational, 72-73
    intonation, 77-79
    points of view, 75-76
    purposes of, 79-80
State abbreviations, 289, 291
Story writing, 236-237, 261
Stress and speaking, 78
Subject of sentence, 21-27, 156, 192-195, 220-
223, 224-225, 228, 229, 264-265, 295-297, 298,
299
Suffixes, 89, 92, 140, 142-143, 148, 292
Symbols, 196-197, 207-216
Synonyms, 200-206
Tall tales, 169, 180-183, 188
Tense in verb phrase, 124-127
Testimonials, 212-217
Time-order sentences, 177, 188, 292
Transforms
    adjective, 297, 304
    compound, 224-229, 302-303
    negative, 294-295, 303
    possessive, 296-297, 304
    question, 264-269
    request, 295, 304
Transitional words, 71, 72, 84, 147, 262
Trite expressions, 116
True statements, recognizing, 214-215, 217
```

1. On which page would you look in order to find information about trite expressions?

   _____

2. How many different types of transforms are to be found in this book?

   _____

3. One form of propaganda is the use of smear words. Where might you find this?

   _____

4. Where would you find information to help you write a story?

   _____

5. Which topic listed in this index seems to be referred to most in this book?

   _____

6. When speaking to a group, you sometimes must do this without planning. This is called improvisation. On which page will you find help?

   _____

© 1981 by The Center for Applied Research in Education, Inc.

Table Mountain, 426
Tablets, clay writing, 9
Tacitus, 140
Tagus River, 109
Taiwan, and its people, 346, 351-352
Tamil language, 302
Tanker, defined, 49
Taoists, 315-316
Tapestry, defined, 172
Tasman, Abel, 439-440
Tasmania, 435
Taxes
   in ancient Egypt, 32
   in Benelus, 202
   in early Russia, 223
   in Middle Ages, 154
   in Roman Empire, 106
   in Russia, 223, 231, 235, 236
Tea
   in Ceylon, 302
   in Indonesia, 378
   in Kenya, 426
Teak
   in Southeast Asia, 366
   in Thailand, 373
Tel Aviv, Israel, 47
Telemachus, 112
Telescope, 173
Television
   in India, 279
Temperature
   and altitude, 389
   ocean, 140-141
   at South Pole, 2
Temples
   in ancient India, 270, 271
   in Bangkok, 372
   Chinese family, 326
   in Laos, 371
   Pantheon, 110
   Parthenon, 89-90
   Solomon's, 36
   in Sumer, 22
Tents, 54, 55
Terraces, 335
Textiles and textile mills
   in China, 350
   in Germany, 212
   in Middle East, 51
   in North Africa, 51
   in Pakistan, 294
   in Republic of South Africa, 425
Thailand and the Thai people, 365
Thames River, 185
Thermometer, 173
Thinking, 172-174

Name _____

Date _____

Look It Up!

You are to look through the index to the left and then answer the questions.

1. On which page would you look to find information about Tasmania?

   _____

2. On which pages would you look to find information about Russian taxes?

   _____

3. In this book, the tea of what countries is discussed?

   _____

4. There are textile mills located in Germany. On what page might you find this?

   _____

5. Where would you find information about the people of Taiwan?

   _____

6. Which topic listed in this index seems to be referred to most in this book?

   _____

7. One of the most famous temples in the world is the Parthenon. On which pages will you find information about it?

   _____

Deep in the Ocean

Name _____

Date _____

Follow the submarine through the ocean. Each time you come to a fish you are to decide whether or not you would find the topic under the fish in an atlas. If you think you would find it in an atlas, copy the circled letter in the space at the bottom of this sheet. If you are correct, the circled letters will spell the ocean in which you have been traveling!

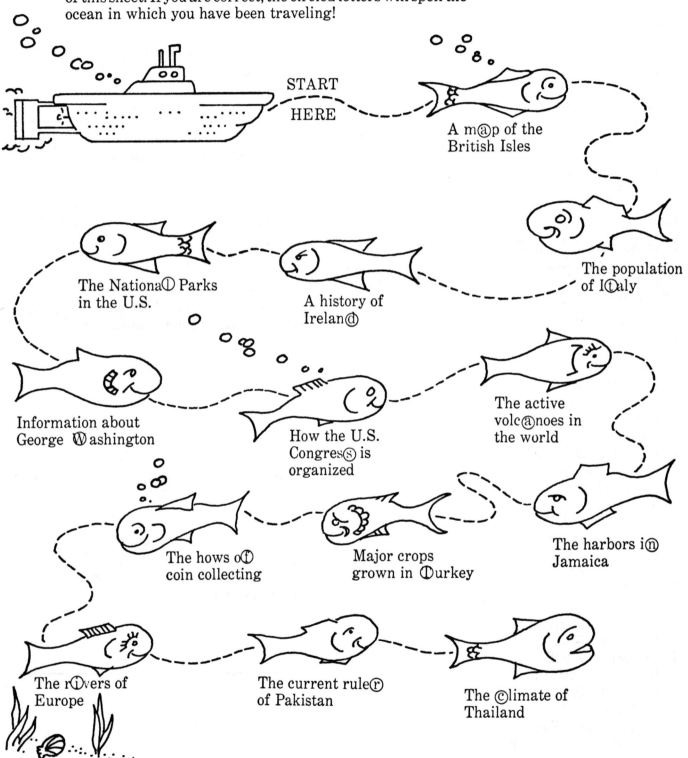

START HERE

A m@p of the British Isles

The population of I(t)aly

The Nationa(l) Parks in the U.S.

A history of Irelan(d)

Information about George (W)ashington

How the U.S. Congres(s) is organized

The active volc@noes in the world

The hows o(f) coin collecting

Major crops grown in (T)urkey

The harbors i(n) Jamaica

The r(i)vers of Europe

The current rule(r) of Pakistan

The (c)limate of Thailand

___ ___ ___ ___ ___ ___ ___

© 1981 by The Center for Applied Research in Education, Inc.

190

Walk Through the Forest

Name _____

Date _____

Follow the path through the woods. Each time you come to a tree you are to decide whether you would find the topic on the tree in an encyclopedia. If you think you would find it in an encyclopedia, copy the circled letter in the space at the bottom of this sheet. If you are correct, the circled letters will spell the kind of trees in this forest!

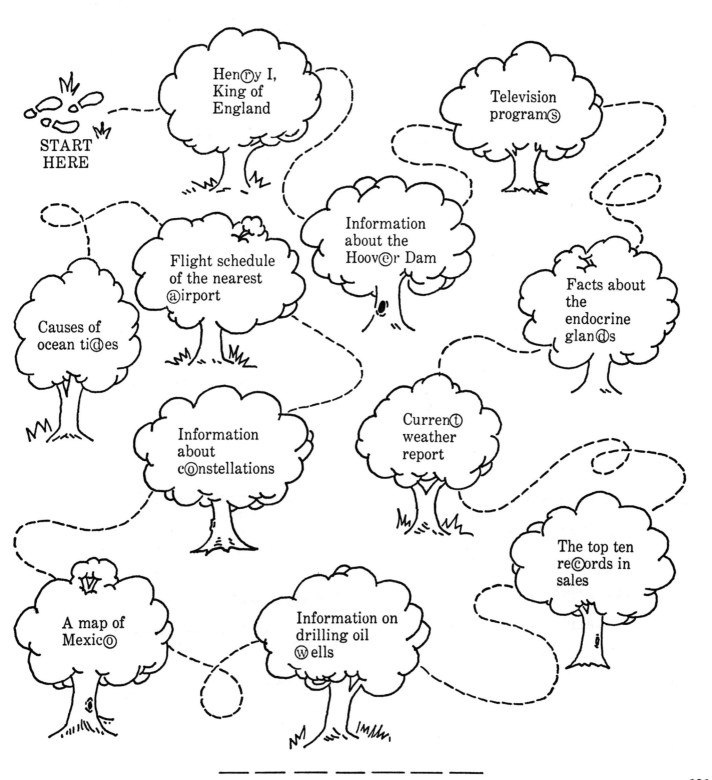

___ ___ ___ ___ ___ ___

191

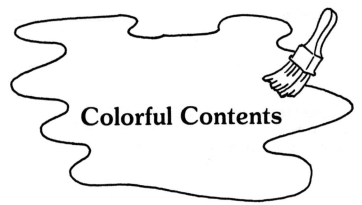
Colorful Contents

Name _____

Date _____

Below are two table of contents puzzles. You are to read each question and decide in which chapter the answer would be found. Write the circled letter in each question next to the appropriate chapter. If you are correct, the circled letters in each puzzle will spell a color.

Puzzle One:

_____ I. How Transportation Affects Our Lives

_____ II. Kinds of Transportation

_____ III. Transportation in Other Lands

_____ IV. Development of Transportation

_____ V. Problems of Transportation

_____ VI. Government and Transportation

What is the cheapest form of f(r)eight transportation?

Why were roads important to a(n)cient empires?

Who is r(e)sponsible for building the roads in the United States?

What are five ways railroads affect (o)ur lives?

How can a country's (g)eography be a problem to transportation?

What is the most important means of p(a)ssenger travel in Japan?

Puzzle Two:

_____ I. Kinds of Animals

_____ II. The Importance of Animals

_____ III. Where Animals Live

_____ IV. Animals' Way of Life

_____ V. Animal Bodies

What animals would you find in the tr(o)pical forests?

What are th(r)ee ways in which animals help plants?

How do salama(n)ders breathe?

What groups of animals are warm-(b)looded?

Ho(w) do animals defend themselves?

The High Jump

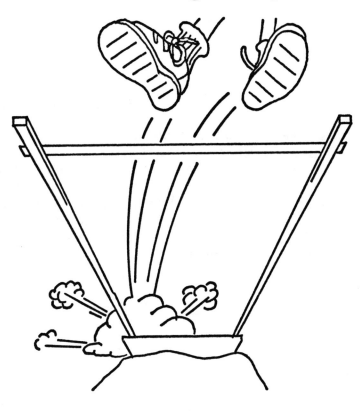

"Wow," yelled Bob. "That's the highest you ever jumped."

"Let's measure it," said Jim, picking himself up.

Bob and Jim were practicing the high jump at the high school field and Jim just made a very high jump. How far do you think it is? Well, there is a way for you to find out! Look below at the pairs of phrases. You are to read each pair and decide which you would find in an atlas. When you decide, write the circled letters in those phrases in the spaces at the bottom of this sheet. If you are correct, these letters will spell the height Jim just jumped.

The ⓕlag of Israel.	(or)	A ⓑrief history of India.
A diⓐgram of the human heart.	(or)	A map of Scⓞtland.
Directions for buildⓘng a go-cart.	(or)	The border between Iraq and Saⓤdi Arabia.
The population of Buⓡma.	(or)	A streeⓣ map of your local city.
The kindⓢ of fish in the oceans.	(or)	The climate in Ⓕinland.
The ⓜost popular TV show.	(or)	The languagⓔ spoken in Kuwait.
The altitudⓔ of Mt. Rainier.	(or)	A diagrⓐm of the solar system.
A review oⓕ best selling books.	(or)	The currenⓣs in the Pacific Ocean.

__ __ __   __ __ __ __

Name _____

Date _____

Help for Jack!

Jack wants to go outside and play with his friends, but his parents have told him he must finish his homework first. He has a few things to look up in the encyclopedia. Unfortunately, some of the information he is looking for cannot be found in the encyclopedia. Maybe you can help him! Below is the list of things Jack must look up. You are to write the word YES next to the things you think he would find in the encyclopedia and NO next to those he would not. When you are finished, you are to copy the circled letters in those things marked YES on the blanks provided at the bottom of this sheet. If you are correct, the circled letters will spell what Jack's friends are playing outside.

_____ Facts about the Wright Ⓑrothers.

_____ The daily weatheⓇ forecast.

_____ Information Ⓐbout Abraham Lincoln.

_____ The Ⓢize of Michigan.

_____ The weekly Ⓣelevision schedule.

_____ Facts about Ⓔlephants.

_____ Information aⒷout tidal waves.

_____ The Ⓓaily news.

_____ TheⒶltitude of the Rocky Mountain Range.

_____ Your school businⒺss plan.

_____ The state fⓁower of Iowa.

_____ Facts about AⓁexander Graham Bell.

___ ___ ___ ___ ___ ___ ___ ___

194

It's Ancient History

Name _____

Date _____

Below is a table of contents. You are to look through it and then answer the questions.

1	Ways of Learning About the World .	1
2	The Beginnings of Civilization ..... Cities of Ancient Sumerians The Ancient Civilization of Egypt	20
3	The Birthplace of Three Faiths .... The Faith of the Jews The Faith of the Christians The Faith of the Moslems	36
4	North Africa and the Middle East Today .... Morocco, Algeria, Tunisia, Libya, Egypt, Syria, Lebanon, Israel, Jordan, The Arabian Peninsula, Iraq, Iran, Turkey	45
5	Ancient Greece	79
6	The Roman Empire	102
7	Modern Southern Europe .... Greece, Italy, Spain and Portugal	114
8	A New Way of Life in Northern Europe .... The Feudal Lords and the Manors The Christian Churches during the Middle Ages Towns and Guilds	140
9	Centuries of Change in Northern Europe .... Changing Ways of Government Changing Ways of Living on the Land Changing Ways of Manufacturing Changing Means of Transportation Religious Changes Changing Ways of Thinking Europeans Discover New Lands	157
10	Northern Europe Today .... The British Isles France The Netherlands, Belgium, Luxembourg, Denmark, Norway, Sweden, Finland, Germany, Austria, Switzerland	178
11	Times Past in Russia	220
12	The U.S.S.R. and Eastern Europe in Recent Times	240

1. On what page does the chapter Ancient Greece begin?

   _____

2. How many chapters are in this book?

   _____

3. On what page does the ninth chapter begin?

   _____

4. What is the title of chapter six?

   _____

5. In which chapter would you look in order to find information about the early Moslem religion?

   _____

6. In which chapter would you look in order to find information about Russian history?

   _____

7. What chapter would have information about transportation in Northern Europe?

   _____

8. How many different Northern European countries are discussed in this book?

   _____

9. In which chapter would you look if you had to answer this question, "What were the important cities of the early Roman Empire?"

   _____

Who Let in the Dog?

Name _____

Date _____

"Oh no!" cried Harvey. "Who let that dog in?" Harvey stood in the center of the library and watched as a dog came running by him.

"Catch him!" he hollered. Well, they finally did catch him, but before they did he managed to knock over two sets of bookshelves. You can help Harvey place the books on the proper shelves by using the Dewey decimal classification. Simply write the book title next to the proper classification numerals. When you are finished, copy the circled letters in the blanks provided at the bottom of this sheet. If you are correct, these letters will spell the kind of dog that caused all of the trouble!

000-099 _____

100-199 _____

200-299 _____

300-399 _____

400-499 _____

500-599 _____

600-699 _____

700-799 _____

800-899 _____

900-999 _____

World Book Encyclopedi@

Early Colonial Tim@s

P@inters of the Twentieth Century

Everyd@y Spanish

Our Suprem@ Court

A @reat Philosophy

Novels of Charles Dicke@s

Our Solar Sys@em

The Wo@ld's Religions

The Buil@ing of a Bridge

___ ___ ___ ___ ___ ___ ___ ___

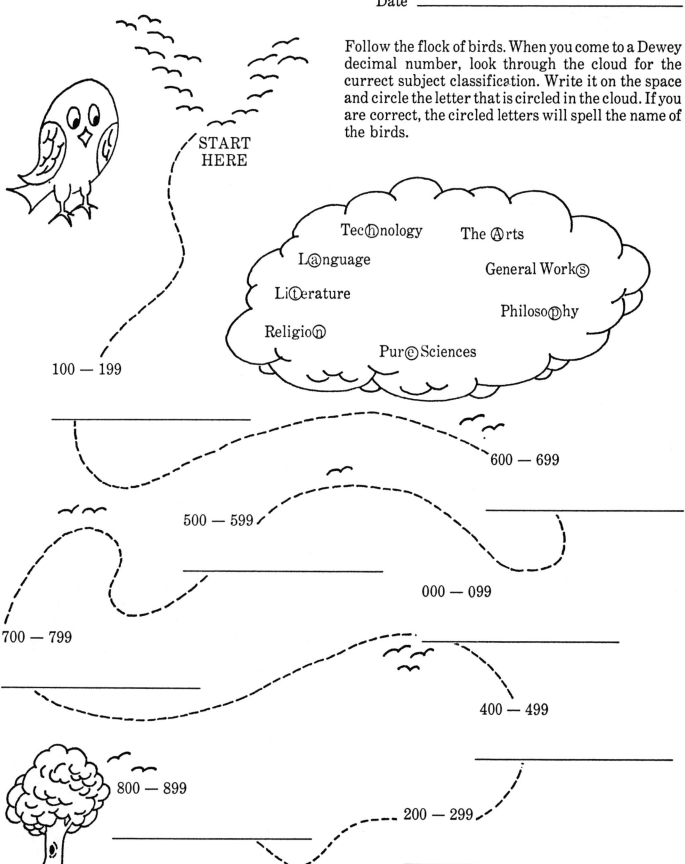

The Mystery at Skull Montain

The Leedys own a cabin up on top of Skull Mountain. They stay in it almost every weekend. On the last few visits they noticed that various things were missing, such as a box of crackers and two candy bars. You can help them solve the mystery of who is taking these items. Simply write the subjects, found in the skull, next to their correct Dewey decimal classification numbers. Be sure to circle the letters that are circled in the skull. If you are correct, these circled letters will spell the name of the thief!

400 — 499 _____

700 — 799 _____

800 — 899 _____

500 — 599 _____

600 — 699 _____

900 — 999 _____

300 — 399 _____

000 — 099 _____

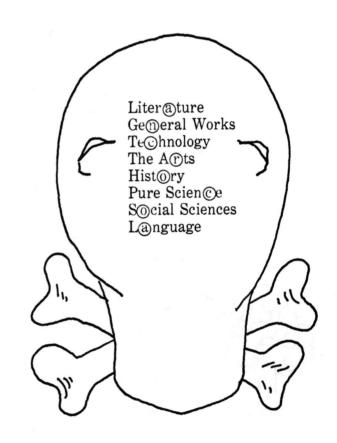

198

Name _____

Date _____

In Chicago!

"Wow!" exclaimed Diane. "Chicago sure is great."

"It sure is," responded Diane's brother, Sam.

The children are with their parents on a vacation in Chicago and are enjoying the sights.

"Oh look at that!" said Diane.

Sam looked high in the sky to where his sister was pointing. What do you think the children are looking at? Well, if you work the following puzzle you will find out. You are to write each book title next to the Dewey decimal classification in which you think you would find the book in a library. Be sure to circle the letters that are circled on this sheet. If you are correct, the circled letters will spell what Diane and Sam are looking at.

600—699 _____   The Civil W(a)r

200—299 _____   Plays of Tennessee William(s)

900—999 _____   (W)ebster's Dictionary

300—399 _____   M(o)dern Music

800—899 _____   Tip (T)op Encyclopedia

000—099 _____   Our Gove(r)nment in Action

700—799 _____   Our Sola(r) System

400—499 _____   The R(e)ligions of India

100—199 _____   New Breakthrough(s) in Medicine

500—599 _____   Curr(e)nt American Philosophy

199

Word Search Puzzle

Name _____

Date _____

Here is a word search puzzle. Hidden among all those letters are words. In order to help you find the words, their definitions are written below the puzzle. If you write the words in the blanks next to their correct definitions, the circled letters will spell a word describing how well you did. Good luck!

```
A B E N C Y C L O P E D I A T J O
T M C D I C T I O N A R Y O B B Z
V X C A R D C A T A L O G M N R C
S U B J E C T C A R D I A A T M
Q U B E F G T I T L E C A R D P O
D G I K M O Q S A T L A S T V X Z
A C E F I C T I O N G I K N P R T
N O N F I C T I O N P Q S R N B A
T X O P Q C D R S G A L M A N A C
U S B A C P E R I O D I C A L S E
T G U I D E L E T T E R S S I B I
```

_ _ Ⓞ _ _ _ _ _   A publication containing statistical and factual information.

Ⓞ _ _ _ _   A book of maps.

Ⓞ _ _ _ _ _ _   _ _ _ _ _ _ _   Letters on each drawer in a card catalog.

_ _ _ _ _ Ⓞ _ _ _   A book filled with definitions.

_ Ⓞ _ _ _ _ _ _ _   Located in card catalogs to help you find books by their titles.

Ⓞ _ _ _ _ _ _   An imaginary story.

_ _ _ Ⓞ _ _ _ _ _ _   A book dealing with factual material.

_ _ _ Ⓞ _ _ _ _ _ _ _ _   A file in which there are library cards for every book in the library.

Ⓞ _ _ _ _ _ _ _ _ _   Magazines and journals found in a library.

_ Ⓞ _ _ _ _ _ _ _ _ _ _   A series of books containing a summary of knowledge.

_ _ _ _ _ _ Ⓞ _ _ _ _   Located in card catalogs to help you find books by their subject.

200

SUPER SHEETS

Did I Hear an S.O.S.?

I thought I heard an S.O.S. coming from you the other day. Perhaps these activity sheets will help?

Your friend,

SUPER SHEETS
To the Rescue!

I thought these activity sheets might come in handy to help you reinforce library and study skills. Hope you find them useful!

Your friend,

Answer Key to Puzzle Sheets

Shipshape: This puzzle sheet is self-correcting. A picture of a ship will be formed if the correct alphabetical order is followed.

A Table of What? The answer to the eight questions are as follows:

1. page 68
2. nine chapters
3. page 96
4. "Staying Safe"
5. Chapter 4, "What Food Does"
6. Chapter 3, "Our Senses"
7. Chapter 9, "Families"
8. Chapter 5, "How We Grow"

Stairway to the Moon: The puzzle is self-correcting. The word JUPITER will be spelled if the puzzle is completed correctly.

Dave's Birthday: The puzzle is self-correcting. The words NINE YEARS OLD will be spelled if the sheet is completed correctly.

The Balloon That Got Away! The puzzle is self-correcting. The words THREE YEARS will be spelled if it is done correctly.

How Do You Know? The answers to the five questions are as follows:

1. pages 25 and 27
2. pages 28-31
3. page 75
4. exercise and families are about equal
5. pages 130-131

Arrange the Books: This puzzle is self-correcting. The words REALLY TREMENDOUS will be spelled if it is completed correctly.

Take a Train Ride: The puzzle is self-correcting. The word CHICAGO will be spelled if the puzzle is completed correctly.

Which Drawer? Answers to this puzzle are as follows:

1. F-I
2. A-Cr
3. O-Rab
4. O-Rab
5. Rac-S
6. O-Rab
7. W-Z
8. F-I
9. A-Cr
10. O-Rab
11. Cu-E
12. Lat-N
13. F-I
14. A-Cr
15. Rac-S

Let's Take a Trip! This puzzle is self-correcting. The word MICHIGAN will be spelled if it is completed correctly.

Ski Jumping: This puzzle is self-correcting. The words LAKE PLACID will be spelled if it is completed correctly.

What Country Are We In? The puzzles are self-correcting. The words BELGIUM and YUGOSLAVIA will be spelled if the puzzles are completed correctly.

Follow the Rainbow: This puzzle is self-correcting. The words IN THE WOODS will be spelled if it is completed correctly.

My Favorite! This puzzle is self-correcting. The word BIRTHDAY will be spelled if it is completed correctly.

Oh No! This puzzle is self-correcting. The words BASEBALL GAME will be spelled if it is completed correctly.

Crossing Death Valley: This puzzle is self-correcting. The words TWO DAYS will be spelled if it is completed correctly.

Symbols of America: The puzzle is self-correcting. The words STARS AND STRIPES, BALD EAGLE, and UNCLE SAM will be spelled if it is completed correctly.

What a Score! This puzzle is self-correcting. The word TWENTY will be spelled if it is completed correctly.

An Artist: This puzzle is self-correcting. The name PICASSO will be spelled if it is completed correctly.

Very Berry: This puzzle is self-correcting. The words APPLES and CHERRY will be spelled if it is completed correctly.

Be a Sport! These puzzles are self-correcting. The words TENNIS and BADMINTON will be spelled if they are completed correctly.

Oh Gosh! This puzzle is self-correcting. The words STAR WARS will be spelled if it is completed correctly.

Suppose You Knew...: This puzzle is self-correcting. The words HORSE, SHEEP, and ROBIN will be spelled if the puzzle is completed correctly.

Presidents Puzzle: These puzzles are self-correcting. The words POLK and HARRISON will be spelled if they are completed correctly.

Dogs...Dogs...Dogs! These puzzles are self-correcting. The words POODLE and COLLIE will be spelled if the puzzles are completed correctly.

Guide Word Puzzle: This puzzle is self-correcting. The words VERY GOOD will be spelled if it is completed correctly.

Tree Mania! These puzzles are self-correcting. The words MAPLE, BIRCH, SPRUCE, and ORANGE will be spelled if they are completed correctly.

High-Rise Apartments: This puzzle is self-correcting. The words TWENTY-SEVEN will be spelled if it is completed correctly.

A Visit to Their Grandparents: The puzzle is self-correcting. The words TREASURE ISLAND FLORIDA will be spelled if it is completed correctly.

Buzz Off! The puzzle is self-correcting. The word GERANIUM will be spelled if it is completed correctly.

The Surprise! These puzzles are self-correcting. The words A BICYCLE and TEN SPEED will be spelled if they are completed correctly.

Great Animals of the Past: This puzzle is self-correcting. The word TYRANNOSAURUS will be spelled if it is completed correctly.

Index Information: The answers to the six questions are as follows:

1. 116
2. six
3. 209-210
4. 236-237, 261
5. subject of sentence
6. 72-73

Look It Up! The answers to the seven questions are as follows:

1. 435
2. 223, 231, 235, 236
3. Ceylon, Indonesia, Kenya
4. 212
5. 346, 351-352
6. Temples
7. 89-90

Deep in the Ocean: The puzzle is self-correcting. The word ATLANTIC will be spelled if the puzzle is completed correctly.

Walk Through the Forest: This puzzle is self-correcting. The word REDWOOD will be spelled if the puzzle is completed correctly.

Colorful Contents: These puzzles are self-correcting. The words ORANGE and BROWN will be spelled if they are completed correctly.

The High Jump: This puzzle is self-correcting. The words FOUR FEET will be spelled if it is completed correctly.

Help for Jack! This puzzle is self-correcting. The word BASEBALL will be spelled if it is completed correctly.

It's Ancient History: The answers to the nine questions are as follows:

1. 79
2. 12 chapters
3. page 157
4. "The Roman Empire"
5. Chapter 3
6. Chapter 11
7. Chapter 9
8. twelve
9. Chapter 6

Who Let in the Dog? The puzzle is self-correcting. The words A GREAT DANE will be spelled if it is completed correctly.

Follow the Flock! The puzzle is self-correcting. The word PHEASANT will be spelled if it is completed correctly.

The Mystery at Skull Mountain: The puzzle is self-correcting. The words A RACCOON will be spelled if it is completed correctly.

In Chicago! The puzzle is self-correcting. The words SEARS TOWER will be spelled if it is completed correctly.

Word Search Puzzle: The puzzle is self-correcting. The word MAGNIFICENT will be spelled if it is completed correctly.

V

Library Skills Games

The games in this section are designed to help you teach and/or reinforce a variety of specific library skills. Most of these library skills games can be played by an individual student or by a small group of youngsters and require little or no supervision. Each game is complete, including a list of materials needed, step-by-step construction directions, and student game directions.

> **NOTE**: Children in the intermediate grades are quite capable of making these games. By forming a small work force of these students, you will be able to make a large number of games within a short time.

You will find many of these games valuable when teaching a unit on library usage or study skills. Once a suitable supply of games is available, teachers can be encouraged to check them out of the resource center for use in their classrooms. A check-out system can be created by simply placing each game in a manila envelope to which a library pocket and card are attached. Mark the name of the game and the skill it reinforces on the envelope and the card.

Following is a list of the games, the skills they reinforce, and suggested grade levels for use.

Game	Library Skill	Grade Level
Key Ring	alphabetization	primary
A Whale of a Good Time	alphabetization	primary
Traveling by Rail	location of fiction books on shelves	primary
Apples, Oranges, and Lemons!	index usage	high primary
Blast Off!	encyclopedia usage	high primary/low intermediate
Grand Prix	alphabetization	high primary/low intermediate
Through the Night Sky	alphabetization	high primary/low intermediate

Library Skills Games

Game	Library Skill	Grade Level
Climb the Mountain	card catalog usage	high primary/low intermediate
Something's Fishy!	table of contents usage	high primary/low intermediate
Pick a Balloon	dictionary usage	high primary/low intermediate
Spin Out	card catalog usage	high primary/low intermediate
Table "Twirl" of Contents	table of contents usage	high primary/intermediate
The Big "E"	encyclopedia usage	high primary/intermediate
Rockets Away!	guide word usage	high primary/intermediate
Sad Sack	guide word usage	high primary/intermediate
Answer the Telephone	alphabetization	intermediate
Match to Win!	table of contents usage	intermediate
Shelve 'Em!	location of fiction books on shelves	intermediate
Who Shelved This?	location of fiction books on shelves	intermediate
Hang It!	atlas usage	intermediate
Crazy Cards	card catalog usage	intermediate
Find the Drawer	card catalog usage	intermediate
Truckin' Down Highway 199	card catalog usage	intermediate
In This Book?	index usage	intermediate
Down Periscope	encyclopedia usage	intermediate
Champ	guide word usage	intermediate
Cecil's Lotto Game	Dewey decimal classification	high intermediate
Which Category?	Dewey decimal classification	high intermediate

Library Skills Games

KEY RING

Skill Reinforced:

alphabetization

Materials Needed:

6 large paper clips
10 sheets each color 3" × 5" posterboard—white, red, green, blue, yellow, orange
hole punch
scissors
felt-tipped pen

Construction Directions:

1. In each of the posterboard pieces cut out a key using the pattern here and punch a single hole in the top.

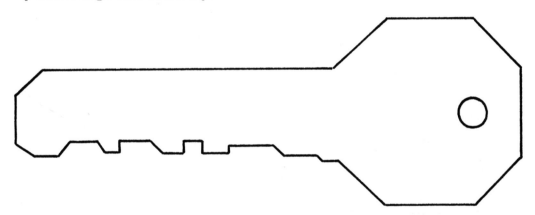

2. Copy each of the following words on a different color key.

   apple   boy
   cow   dog
   eat   fit
   girl   house
   ink   jam

3. Bend the paper clips so they look like this.

Game Play:

This game is for two to six players.

1. Each player selects a set of color keys and a key ring (paper clip), and places them, face down, in front of him.
2. At a signal all players turn over their keys and put them on their key rings in alphabetical order. The first player to do this correctly is the winner.

Library Skills Games

A WHALE OF A GOOD TIME

Skill Reinforced:

alphabetization

Materials Needed:

10 sheets 9" × 7" gray posterboard
5 pairs of shoelaces
scissors
felt-tipped pen
tape
hole punch

Construction Directions:

1. Cut and mark each posterboard piece by using an enlargement of the whale pattern shown here. Punch holes in each whale.

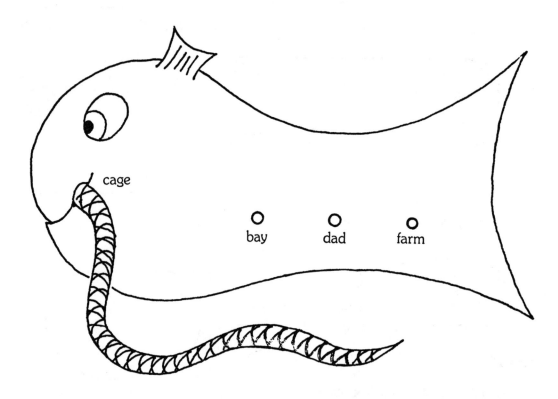

2. Attach each shoelace by putting it through the mouth hole and taping it to the underside of the game piece.

Library Skills Games

3. Print each group of four words shown here on each whale. Place each word in the left column on the whale's head and each of the other three words below a hole on the whale's belly. Draw a circle around the back of the hole above the correct choice.

cage	boy dad farm	sand	my ten very	meet	rug nine hat
few	keep go did	few	ham day land	lake	nail race kick
rain	take sad pack	key	door made red	now	too spot my
pen	right dark tell				

Game Play:

This game is for one player.

1. Choose one of the whales and read the word on the head.
2. Now find a word on the belly that appears before the head word in a dictionary, and place the shoelace through the hole next to that word.
3. When you are finished with all of the whales, turn the pieces over for the self-check.

Library Skills Games

TRAVELING BY RAIL

Skill Reinforced:

location of fiction books on shelves

Materials Needed:

1 sheet of 4½″ × 2½″ gray posterboard
9 sheets of 4″ × 3″ gray posterboard
scissors
felt-tipped pen

Construction Directions:

1. Cut the larger posterboard piece using the engine pattern shown here.

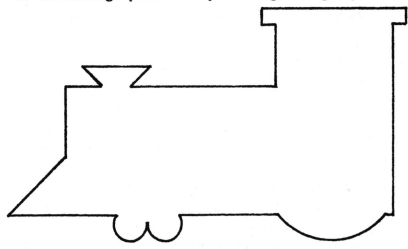

2. Cut the smaller posterboard pieces using the train car pattern shown here.

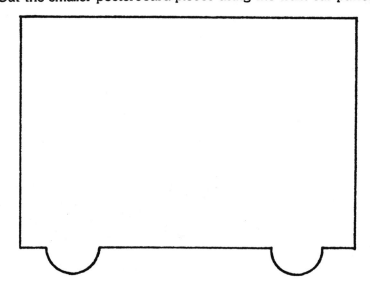

Library Skills Games

3. Print the following title and author on the engine.

    Jenny's Revenge by Anne Baldwin

4. Print each of the following title and author pairs on a different train car. Print the corresponding numerals on the backs of the cars.

    (2) *Petunia* by Roger Duvoisin
    (3) *Little Toot* by Hardie Gramatky
    (4) *Swimmy* by Leo Lionni
    (5) *George and Martha* by James Marshall
    (6) *Eli* by Bill Peet
    (7) *Nothing Ever Happens on My Block* by Ellen Raskin
    (8) *Where the Wild Things Are* by Maurice Sendak
    (9) *Thy Friend, Obadiah* by Brinton Turkle
    (10) *Ira Sleeps Over* by Bernard Waber

Game Play:

This game is for one player.

1. Find the engine and place it on the left-hand side of your desk. Now turn the cars so that they are face up.
2. Each train car has a book title and author on it. You are to attach the cars to the engine by putting them in the same order in which you would find the real books on a library shelf. That is, alphabetically, according to the author's last name and then the title.
3. When you are finished, you may turn over the pieces for the numbers that will tell you how you did.

Library Skills Games

APPLES, ORANGES, AND LEMONS!

Skill Reinforced:

index usage

Materials Needed:

3 sheets 9" × 11" green posterboard
4 sheets 2½" × 2½" posterboard of each color—red, orange, yellow
scissors
felt-tipped pen

Construction Directions:

1. Cut and mark the green posterboard pieces using an enlargement of the tree pattern shown here.

Library Skills Games

2. Cut the red posterboard pieces using the apple pattern shown here.

3. Print each of the following index entries on a different apple. Mark the corresponding numerals on the backs.
   (1) Fish, 23, 31
   (2) Flight:
       of mammals, 20
       of birds, 115
   (3) Floods, 42
   (4) Flowers, 13, 43

4. Cut the orange posterboard pieces using the orange pattern shown here.

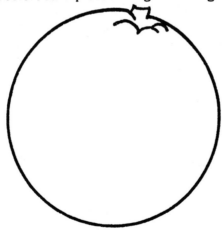

5. Print each of the following index entries on a different orange. Mark the corresponding numerals on the backs.
   (1) Middle East, 174
   (2) Migration
       of birds, 10
       of butterflies, 30
   (3) Minerals, 44, 95
   (4) Minnesota, 152

213

6. Cut the yellow posterboard pieces using the lemon pattern shown here.

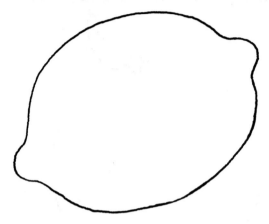

7. Print each of the following index entries on a different lemon. Mark the corresponding numerals on the back.
    (1) Toad, 12
    (2) Toadstool, 134
    (3) Tobacco, 124
    (4) Trees
        evolution of, 49

Game Play:

This game is for one player.
1. Place the trees on your desk. Separate the kinds of fruit into three stacks making sure the index entries are face up.
2. Now place the fruit on the trees in the correct order that they would be found in an index. When you are finished turn over the fruit for the self-check numerals.

Library Skills Games

BLAST OFF!

Skill Reinforced:

encyclopedia usage

Materials Needed:

1 sheet of 8" × 11" red posterboard
scissors
felt-tipped pen

Construction Directions:

Cut and mark the posterboard using the following rocket pattern. Be sure to cut on the broken lines.

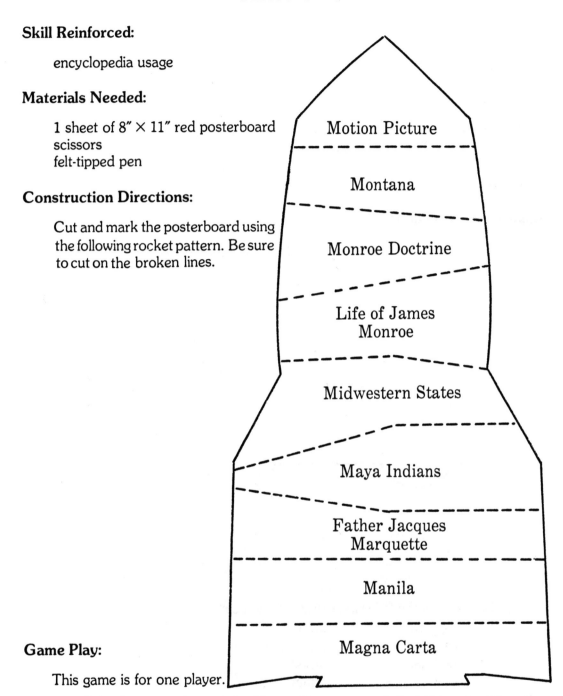

Game Play:

This game is for one player.

1. Turn the game pieces right side up so you can read all of the entries. These are all things you could find in an encyclopedia. You are to put them in the same order as you would expect to find them in an encyclopedia. Put the first one at the bottom of your desk and continue to build on top of it.
2. If you are correct, the puzzle pieces will form a rocket.

Library Skills Games

GRAND PRIX

Skill Reinforced:

alphabetization

Materials Needed:

4 sheets 8" X 15" red posterboard
16 sheets 4" X 2½" white posterboard
scissors
felt-tipped pen

Construction Directions:

1. Cut each of the white posterboard pieces using the race car shape shown here.

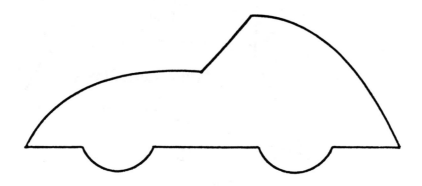

2. Print one of the following words on each car.

applause	array
assembly	attachment
applicant	arrest
asset	attain
apply	arrive
assignment	attend
appose	arrow
associate	attitude

3. To make gameboards, trace nine cars on the red posterboard pieces as shown in the illustration. Use one of the car cutouts as a pattern.

Library Skills Games

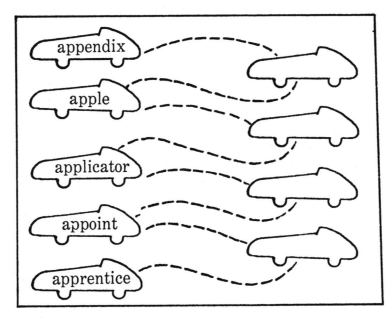

4. Print one of the following lists of words on each gameboard. Leave the cards on the right side of each gameboard blank.

Word List 1	Word List 2	Word List 3	Word List 4
appendix	arrange	assemble	attach
apple	arrears	assent	attack
applicator	arrival	assign	attempt
appoint	arrogant	assist	attention
apprentice	arson	association	attraction

Game Play:

This game is for two to four players.

1. Each player chooses a gameboard and places it in front of him.
2. All of the individual word-cards are dealt to the players. Be sure the cars are face down. Players should not be able to see the words on each other's cards.
3. Players now look at the cars in their hands. If their hands include any words that can be placed in alphabetical order between two of the words listed on the left of the gameboard, they should place these words on the appropriate blank cars on the right of the board.
4. The dealer begins the game by holding out the cars in his or her hand, word side down, to the player to his/her left. This player must take one of these cars. He/she must not show the word to any other player. If the word will fit in the alphabetical order on her gameboard, she places it on the appropriate blank car. If not, she simply adds it to the cars in her hand and continues the game by holding out her cars, word side down, to the player to her left.
5. The game continues in this manner. The first player who fills in the blank cars correctly is the winner.

Library Skills Games

THROUGH THE NIGHT SKY

Skill Reinforced:

alphabetization

Materials Needed:

5 sheets 11" × 8½" blue posterboard
8 sheets 2¾" × 2½" posterboard for each color—white, red, yellow, orange, and green
scissors
felt-tipped pen

Construction Directions:

1. Copy an enlargement of the gameboard shown here on the five sheets of blue posterboard.

2. Cut the small posterboard pieces into star shapes using the following star pattern.

218

Library Skills Games

3. Copy each of the following words on a different color star.
    dial
    dialect
    diameter
    diamond
    diaper
    diary
    dictate
    diet

Game Play:

This game is for two to five players.

1. Each player selects a gameboard and eight stars of the same color.
2. When all players are ready, one player says "begin." At this signal, all players attempt to place their stars on the gameboard in alphabetical order. The first to do this correctly is the winner.

Library Skills Games

CLIMB THE MOUNTAIN

Skill Reinforced:

card catalog usage

Materials Needed:

1 sheet of 8" × 11" white posterboard
9 sheets of 1" × 2" red posterboard
scissors
felt-tipped pen

Construction Directions:

1. Cut and mark the white posterboard using an enlargement of the mountain pattern shown here.

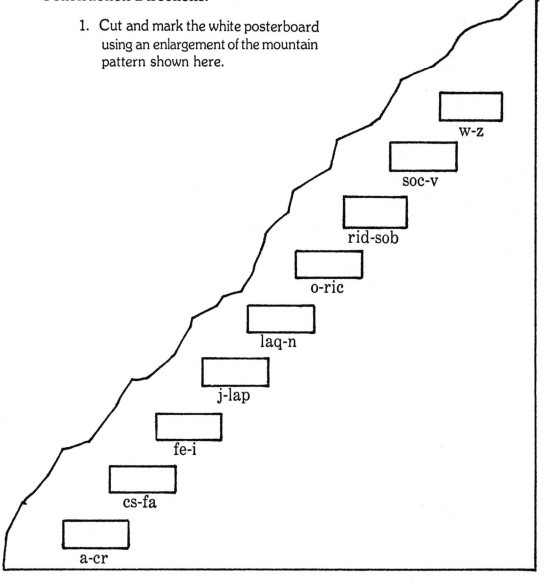

Library Skills Games

2. Print each of the following book titles on a different red card. Print the corresponding guide letters on the back of each card.

   Call It Courage (A-Cr)
   Ellen Grae (Cs-Fa)
   Incident at Hawk's Hill (Fe-I)
   The Lantern Bearers (J-Lap)
   The Little Fishes (Laq-N)
   Pulga (O-Ric)
   The Slave Dancer (Rid-Sob)
   Summer of My German Soldier (Soc-V)
   The Witch's Brat (W-Z)

Game Play:

This game is for one player.

1. Place the mountain on your desk so you can read the letters. They are similar to the guide letters on the drawers of a card catalog.
2. Place the red cards so you can read all of the book titles. At the bottom of the mountain are the letters A-Cr. Can you find a book title that would go in this drawer? Place it on the square above these letters. Continue doing this as you climb the mountain.
3. When you are finished, you may turn over the pieces for the self-check.

Library Skills Games

SOMETHING'S FISHY!

Skill Reinforced:

table of contents usage

Materials Needed:

5 sheets of 6" × 8" yellow posterboard
scissors
felt-tipped pen

Construction Directions:

1. Cut and mark the posterboard pieces using the fish pattern shown on page 223.
2. Print the following chapter titles on the fish heads, as shown in the illustration, and the corresponding numerals on the back of the pieces.
    - (1) "Children and Families"
    - (2) "Shelter for the Families"
    - (3) "Food for the Families"
    - (4) "Clothes for the Families"
    - (5) "The United States"
3. Print the following questions on the fish tails, as shown in the illustration, and the corresponding numerals on the back of the pieces.
    - (1) How are children the same?
    - (2) Why does your family need a house?
    - (3) How does your family get food?
    - (4) Why do people choose different kinds of clothes?
    - (5) What does our country look like where you live?

Game Play:

This game is for one player.

1. Turn the pieces right side up and separate them into two groups: fish heads and fish tails.
2. Now read one of the questions. Look through the chapter titles and find one in which you think you might find the answer to this question. Place these two pieces together so they form a fish. Continue doing this with all of the pieces.
3. When you are finished, turn over the pieces for the self-check numerals.

Library Skills Games

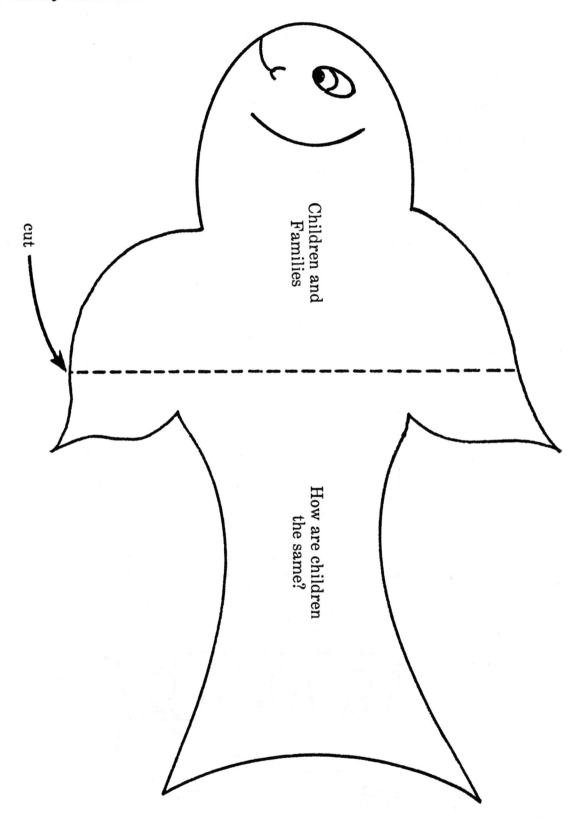

Library Skills Games

PICK A BALLOON

Skill Reinforced:

dictionary usage

Materials Needed:

10 sheets 6" × 7" red posterboard
scissors
felt-tipped pen

Construction Directions:

1. Cut, fold and mark the posterboard pieces as shown here.

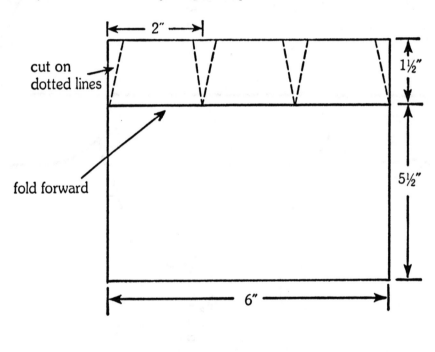

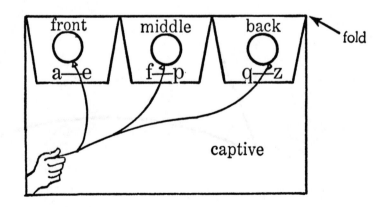

Library Skills Games

2. Print each of the following words on a different gameboard, as shown in the illustration, and write CORRECT under the appropriate flap.

(front)	(middle)	(back)
captive	industry	swim
discomfort	honor	than
blend	monopoly	water
approval		

Game Play:

This game is for one player.

1. Choose a gameboard and read the word. Do you think you would find it in the front, middle, or back part of your dictionary?
2. When you think you know, lift up that flap to check for the correct answer.

Library Skills Games

SPIN OUT

Skill Reinforced:

card catalog usage

Materials Needed:

1 sheet 6" × 6" white posterboard
1 sheet 5" × 1" black posterboard
paper fastener
30 sheets 2½" × 3" yellow posterboard
scissors
felt-tipped pen

Construction Directions:

1. Cut the black posterboard and attach it with a paper fastener as a spinner to the white sheet as shown here. Mark the white sheet as shown.

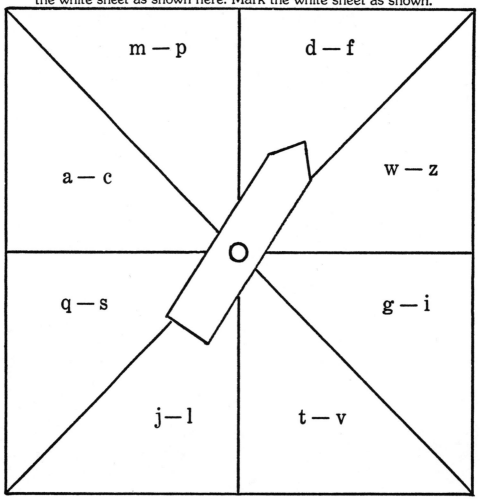

Library Skills Games

2. Copy each of the following words on a different yellow card.

Burma	magic
astronaut	facing
natural history	Finland
England	yellow fever
water	horse
igloo	Uganda
television	jogging
kangaroo	Quaker
clown	mountain
pumpkin	bloodhound
frogmen	Europe
weather	hurricane
game	valentine
turkey	revolution
lamb	spring

Game Play:

This game is for two to five players.

1. One player deals all the yellow cards to the players.
2. The dealer now spins. If he has a card with a word that is alphabetically between the letters he spun, he may discard it. If not, the next player takes his spin.
3. The game continues in this manner until one player has discarded all of his cards. That player is the winner.

Library Skills Games

TABLE "TWIRL" OF CONTENTS

Skills Reinforced:

table of contents usage

Materials Needed:

5 sheets of 4" × 6" red posterboard
5 circles with 4" diameters, white posterboard
5 paper fasteners
scissors
felt-tipped pen

Construction Directions:

1. Cut a 2" × ½" window in each of the red posterboard pieces and fasten a circle to each one as shown here.

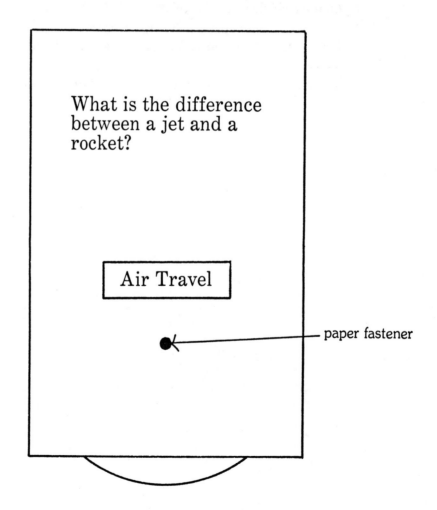

Library Skills Games

2. Print the following questions on the posterboard pieces and the chapter heading groups on the circle, as shown in the illustration. Simply turn the circle to write in all three chapter headings. Print the correct answer on the back of each card.

   What is the difference between a jet and a rocket?
   > Air Travel
   > The Earth's Neighbors
   > Weather

   From what do we get vitamin A?
   > The How of Flowers
   > Heating our Homes
   > Food for Energy

   How do water animals get oxygen?
   > Boats
   > Woodland Animals
   > Life in Ponds and Streams

   What kind of houses do squirrels build?
   > Scientists
   > Boats
   > Woodland Animals

   How far is the moon from the earth?
   > Weather
   > The Earth's Neighbors
   > Air Travel

Game Play:

This game is for one player.

1. Look at the question on one of the cards. If you were to look in a book for the answer to this question, in which chapter would you look? Turn the circle and see if you can figure out which chapter is correct.
2. For a self-check, look at the back of the game card.

Library Skills Games

THE BIG "E"

Skill Reinforced:

encyclopedia usage

Materials Needed:

5 sheets of 6" × 6" yellow posterboard
5 shoelaces
scissors
felt-tipped pen
hole punch

Construction Directions:

1. Cut and mark the posterboard pieces using the E pattern shown here.

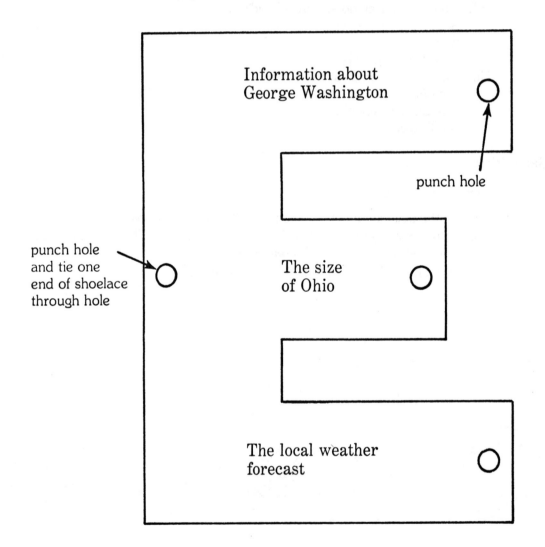

230

Library Skills Games

2. Print the following groups of sentences on the E's as shown in the illustration. Mark the back of the correct circle.

   (A) Information about George Washington
   The size of Ohio
   The local weather forecast

   (B) The depths of the Pacific Ocean
   The latest movies being produced
   Facts about making movies

   (C) Height of the Empire State Building
   Current television programs
   Facts about dogs

   (D) Items on sale at the food store
   Information about trees
   Currents in the oceans

   (E) Facts about Thomas Edison
   How the U.S. space program began
   The daily news

Game Play:

This game is for one player.

1. Look at one of the big E's. Which information wouldn't you expect to find in an encyclopedia?
2. Place the shoelace through the hole next to that information. Now turn over the E. If the hole is marked you are correct. Continue doing this with all of the E's.

Library Skills Games

ROCKETS AWAY!

Skill Reinforced:

guide word usage

Materials Needed:

5 sheets 8" × 8" corrugated cardboard
24 sheets 3" X 6" red posterboard
scissors
felt-tipped pen

Construction Directions:

1. Cut 3½" slits in the corrugated gameboards as shown here.

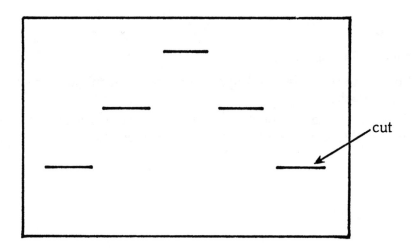

2. Mark and cut the red posterboard pieces using the rocket pattern shown on page 233. Draw a dotted line down the center of each rocket.

Library Skills Games

3. Print each pair of the following guide words and corresponding word on one of the rockets. The guide words should be printed on one side of the dotted line and the corresponding word on the other.

nail — name	naive
nape — narrate	narcotic
narrow — nasty	nasal
nation — navigate	nature
navy — neat	near
necessity — need	neck
needle — neglect	negative
neighbor — neon	neither
nephew — nervous	nerve
nest—neutral	net
never — news	new
nice — niece	nickel
night — nine	nimble
no — noble	nobility
nobody — noise	nod
noisy — nominal	nomad
nominate — nonsense	none
noodle — normal	noon
north — nose	northern
not — notary	notable
notch — nothing	note
notice — noun	notify
nourish — now	novel
nozzle — number	nudge

4. Divide the rocket by cutting along the dotted lines.

Library Skills Games

Game Play:

This game is for two to five players.

1. Separate the rocket pieces and place the right sides of the rockets in one stack and the left sides in another. All playing pieces should be placed face down in the center of the playing area. Each player receives a heavy gameboard and then selects five *left* pocket halves without looking at the words. These are placed in each of the five slots in their gameboards. Players must not show their rockets to each other.

2. All of the right rocket halves are now dealt out to the players. Be sure that they are face down.

3. All players should look through the rocket halves in their hands and try to match them with the halves in their gameboard. If any of the single words fit alphabetically between the guide words, players should fit them together on their gameboards.

4. The player who dealt the rocket halves begins by holding out his rocket halves, word side down, to the player on his left who must take one of the pieces without showing it to any other player. If it will fit alphabetically between any of the guide words in her gameboard, she places it in that slot. If not, she simply adds it to the playing pieces already in her hand and continues the game by holding out her rocket halves, wordside down, to the player on her left.

5. The game continues in this manner until one of the players has five complete rockets. That player is the winner

Library Skills Games

SAD SACK

Skill Reinforced:

guide word usage

Materials Needed:

21 sheets 3" × 4" yellow posterboard
20 sheets 3" × 4" red posterboard
felt-tipped pen

Construction Directions:

1. Mark each of the following word pairs on a different yellow card.

    antelope — antic
    annual — another
    antique — apathy
    apogee — apparent
    appear — apply
    apron — arbitrate
    archery — area
    arena — arise
    arm — arrange
    arsenal — articulate
    ascribe — aspire
    assess — assort
    assume — astray
    asunder — athlete
    atmosphere — attest
    auction — author
    autograph — autumn
    avenge — await
    aware — axis
    about — academy

2. Copy each of the following words on a different red card.

anoint	anthem
antler	apostrophe
applaud	aqueduct
arctic	argue
army	arson
ask	assign
aster	at
attack	audit
automobile	average
awe	abrupt

3. Copy the following "Sad Sack" on one of the yellow cards.

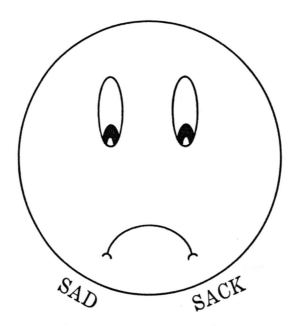

Game Play:

This game is for two to four players.

1. A player deals out all of the cards. Players should not let other players see their cards.
2. All players should look through their cards to find single words on their red cards that fit between any of their pairs of guide words. If they have them, they lay them down.
3. The player who dealt the cards begins by holding out his cards, face down, to the player on his left. This player must take one of the cards. She should not show it to any other player. If it matches another of her cards, she lays them down. If not, she adds it to the cards in her hand and continues the game by holding out the cards to the player on her left.
4. The game continues until all cards are paired. The player left holding the "Sad Sack" card is the loser and receives an "S". When a player has accumulated all the letters in the words "Sad Sack," he is out of the game. The last player remaining is the winner.

Library Skills Games

ANSWER THE TELEPHONE

Skill Reinforced:

alphabetization

Materials Needed:

a local telephone directory
1 sheet 16" × 20" white posterboard
30 sheets 3" × 4" red posterboard
colored gummed circles
felt-tipped pen
game markers

Construction Directions:

1. Mark the white gameboard as shown here. Attach the gummed circles as indicated.

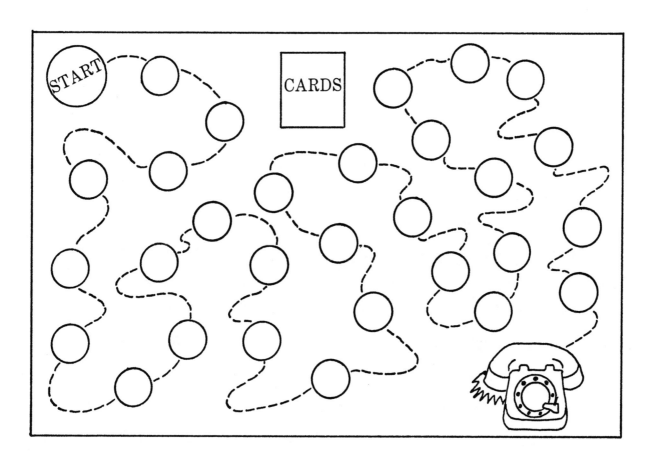

2. Using your local telephone directory as a guide, write a different question on each of the thirty red cards. For example:

> Your mother has gone to Smith's Department Store. What number would you dial if you needed to talk to her?
>
> You must call your dad at work. He teaches at Washington Junior High School. What is the number?
>
> You need some information about your stamp collection. Call Joe's Stamps and Coins. What is the number?

Game Play:

This game is for two to five players.

1. Each player places his/her marker on **Start**. The first player takes the top card. If he can find the number in the telephone book he moves one circle. If not, he stays where he is and the next player takes her turn.
2. The first player to reach the telephone is the winner.

Library Skills Games

MATCH TO WIN!

Skill Reinforced:

table of contents usage

Materials Needed:

3 egg cartons
18 sheets 2" × 4" white posterboard
18 sheets 2" × 2½" red posterboard
scissors
felt-tipped pen

Construction Directions:

1. Cut the egg cartons lengthwise down the center so that there is a row of six humps when each half is turned over. Now cut a crosswise slit in each hump.
2. Print one of the following chapter headings on each white posterboard piece as shown here.

Library Skills Games

> Measuring Things
> Traveling Safely
> Looking at the Stars
> Eating for Good Health
> Growing Plants
> Measuring Changes in the Weather
> Electricity Working for Us
> How Animals Live Together
> Mountains, Rocks and Minerals
> Light, Color and Radiant Energy
> Using Fire, Fuels and Heat
> Your Blood System in Action
> The Breathing System in Action
> The Beginnings of Civilization
> The Birthplace of Three Faiths
> The Middle East Today
> Ancient Greece
> The Roman Empire

3. Print one of the following questions on each red posterboard piece.

> How would you measure ingredients for cupcakes?
> Why do some people have more accidents than others?
> How do telescopes help astronomers?
> How does food change in our stomachs?
> How do plants protect themselves?
> What makes the wind blow?
> Explain what a dry cell is.
> What kinds of animals give no care to their young?
> What are ways in which volcanoes build up the earth's surface?
> Why should you wear cloth of light color in the summer?
> How is fuel burned in an automobile engine?
> What task do red corpuscles perform for your body?
> How many air sacs are found in the lungs?
> How did early Egyptians farm?
> What is the holy city of the Moslems?
> What are the advantages of oil pipelines in the Middle East?
> Why did the early Greeks learn about the stars?
> What two rivers formed the northern boundary of the Roman Empire?

Game Play:

This game can be played by two or three players.

1. Each player places an egg carton (upside down) in front of him.
2. One player deals out six white cards to each player, each card to be placed in a slit in the egg carton holder, one card per slit. The red cards are placed face down in a stack in the center of the playing area.

Library Skills Games

3. The first player takes the top red card and reads the question written on it. She then checks to see whether the answer can be found in any of the chapters in her holder. If she finds one, she inserts the red card in the slit with the white chapter card.
4. If the player is unable to use the card, she discards the red card placing it question side up next to the stack of red cards in the center of the playing area.
5. The next player continues the game following in the same pattern.
6. The first player to match six red cards with his six white cards is the winner. If all the red cards in the original stack have been picked and there is still no winner, the red cards that have not been matched are turned over and the game continues.

Library Skills Games

SHELVE 'EM!

Skill Reinforced:

location of fiction books on shelves

Materials Needed:

12 sheets 1″ × 8″ posterboard (various colors)
felt-tipped pen

Construction Directions:

1. Mark the sheets of posterboard to resemble book spines as shown here.

2. Print each of the following titles and authors on a book spine. Mark the corresponding numerals on the backs of the pieces.

(1) *Are You in the House Alone?* by Richard Peck
(2) *Soup* by Robert Peck
(3) *Soup and Me* by Robert Peck
(4) *Soup for President* by Robert Peck
(5) *The Edge of Next Year* by Mary Stolz
(6) *Ferris Wheel* by Mary Stolz
(7) *Leap Before You Look* by Mary Stolz
(8) *Blue Fin* by Colin Thiele
(9) *Fire in the Stone* by Colin Thiele
(10) *The Hammerhead* by Colin Thiele
(11) *Ludell* by Brenda Wilkinson
(12) *Ludell and Willie* by Brenda Wilkinson

Game Play:

This game is for one player.
1. Turn the book spines so that you can read all of the book titles and authors' names. You are to place the spines in the same order in which you would find the books on a library shelf.
2. If you are correct, the numerals on the book backs will be in the correct order.

Library Skills Games

WHO SHELVED THIS?

Skill Reinforced:

location of fiction books on shelves

Materials Needed:

6 sheets 10" × 5" green posterboard
scissors
felt-tipped pen

Construction Directions:

1. Cut and fold the posterboard pieces as shown here.

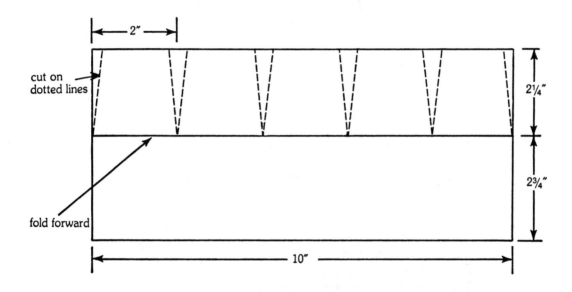

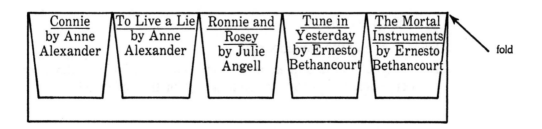

Library Skills Games

2. Print the following sets of authors and book titles on the six gameboards as shown in the illustration. Print the word CORRECT under the flap of the book that is out of the proper order (noted here by an asterisk).

    Connie by Anne Alexander
    To Live a Lie by Anne Alexander
    Ronnie and Rosey by Julie Angell
    Tune in Yesterday by Ernesto Bethancourt
    *The Mortal Instruments by Ernesto Bethancourt

    A Month of Sundays by Rose Blue
    Then Again Maybe I Won't by Judy Blume
    *Tales of a Fourth Grade Nothing by Judy Blume
    Devilhorn by Frank Bonham
    City of Darkness by Ben Bova

    Johnny May by Robbie Branscum
    Me and Jim Luke by Robbie Branscum
    Toby, Granny and George by Robbie Branscum
    *Three Buckets of Daylight by Robbie Branscum
    Uncle Mike's Boy by Jerome Brooks

    *Nobody Has to Be a Kid Forever by Hila Colman
    Pinch by Larry Callen
    Ramona the Pest by Beverly Cleary
    Ellen Grae by Vera & Bill Cleaver
    Grover by Vera & Bill Cleaver

    A Dance to Still Music by Barbara Corcoran
    This Is a Recording by Barbara Corcoran
    Hew Against the Grain by Betty Sue Cummings
    *The Cat Ate My Gymsuit by Paula Danzinger
    The Dangerous Game by Milton Dank

    Across Five Aprils by Irene Hunt
    *William by Irene Hunt
    The Lottery Rose by Irene Hunt
    A Stranger Came Ashore by Mollie Hunter
    Gentlehands by M. E. Kerr

Game Play:

This game is for one player.

1. Choose one of the gameboards.
2. Read the authors and titles on the flaps. Can you find one that is out of the correct order? If you can, lift up that flap for the self-check.

Library Skills Games

HANG IT!

Skill Reinforced:

atlas usage

Materials Needed:

4 potato chip cans (or other can)
Con-Tact paper (colorful design)
20 paper clips
29 posterboard circles—2" diameter
felt-tipped pen
tape
hole punch

Construction Directions:

1. Cover the potato chip cans with the Con-Tact paper.
2. Shape the paper clips into hooks using the pattern shown here and hang five on each can, securing each one with tape on the inside of the can.

3. Punch a hole near the top of each posterboard circle. Now copy each of the following on a different circle.

    A history of Australia
    The presidents of the United States
    The governmental leader of Algeria
    Current religious leaders in New Zealand
    The rotations of the planets in our solar system
    A map showing the different constellations
    A diagram of the workings of a steam engine
    The average depth of the Mediterranean Sea
    A list of the world's largest islands
    The length of the Nile River
    The height of the Yosemite waterfall
    A listing of the world's largest lakes
    A map showing the major forests of the world
    A map of the world
    A map showing the U.S.-Canadian border
    The population of Colorado

The flag of California
The date Kentucky became a state
The capital of Ohio
Major products of North Carolina
Information about our national parks
A map showing the location of our national parks
Information about the battlefields of the Civil War
The major cities in Quebec, Canada
A map of the St. Lawrence River
The language spoken in Mexico
Religions in Trinidad
The climate in Jamaica
A map showing the Panama Canal

Game Play:

This game is for two to four players.

1. Each player receives a "Hang It" can. The circles are placed face down in a stack in the center of the playing area.
2. The first player takes a circle and reads the statement. If she thinks that she could find that information in an atlas she "hangs it" on her can. If not, she places the circle on the bottom of the stack.
3. The next player continues the game in the same manner.
4. The first player to hang five circles on the can is the winner.

Library Skills Games

CRAZY CARDS

Skill Reinforced:

card catalog usage

Materials Needed:

8 sheets of 4" × 5" yellow posterboard
scissors
felt-tipped pen

Construction Directions:

1. Cut and fold the posterboard pieces as shown here.

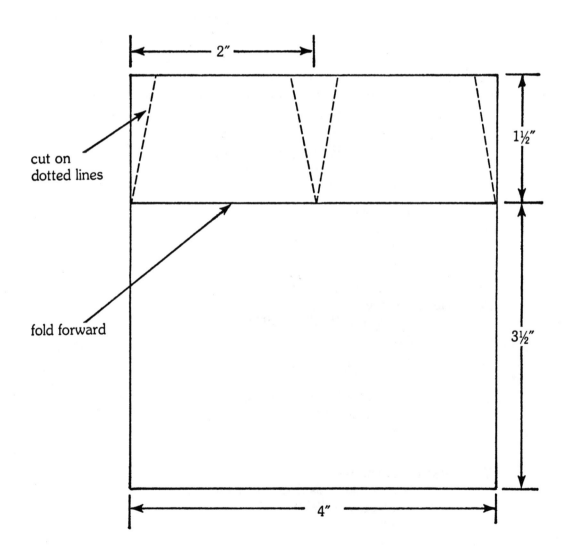

247

Library Skills Games

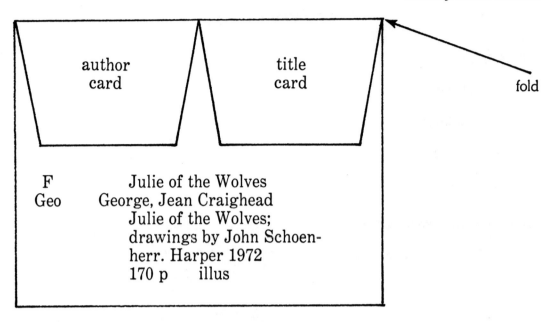

2. Print the following book information on the cards, as shown in the illustration, and draw a star under the correct flap for author card or title card.

    F   Julie of the Wolves
    Geo   George, Jean Craighead
              Julie of the Wolves; drawings by
               John Schoenherr. Harper 1972
               170 p   illus

    F   Mia Alone
    Bec   Beckman, Gunnel
              Mia Alone; Viking 1975
              124 p

    F   The Swing
    Han   Hanlon, Emily
              The Swing; Bradbury 1979
              209 p

    F   The Worst Hound Around
    Dra   Draper, Cena C.
              The Worst Hound Around;
              Westminster 1979
              115 p

    F
    Van   Van Leeuwen, Jean
              Seems Like This Road Goes On
              Forever; Dial 1979
              214 p

Library Skills Games

     F
Gar   Garrigue, Sheila
             Between Friends; Bradbury
             1978
             160 p

     F
Fit   Fitzhugh, Louise
             Sport; Delacorte 1979
             218 p

     F
Org   Orgel, Doris
             The Devil in Vienna; Dial
             1978
             246 p

Game Play:

This game is for one player.

1. Be sure the flaps are down. Read the catalog card. Is this a title card or an author card?
2. When you think you know, lift the flap for the correct answer.

Library Skills Games

FIND THE DRAWER

Skill Reinforced:

card catalog usage

Materials Needed:

5 pieces 12" × 12" brown posterboard
20 pieces 2½" × 3" white posterboard
scissors
felt-tipped pen

Construction Directions:

1. Cut 3" slits in the four brown posterboard pieces using an enlargement of the gameboard pattern shown here.

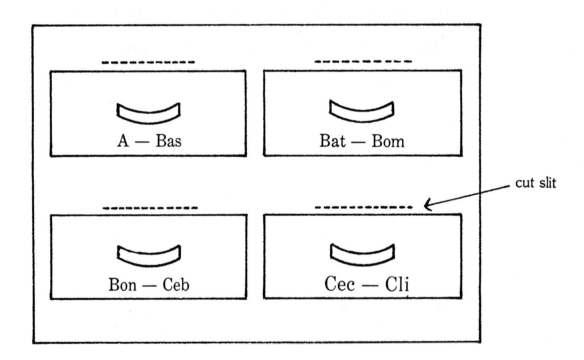

Library Skills Games

2. On each of the brown drawer posterboard pieces, print one of the guide letter groups as shown in the illustration.

Letter Group 1	Letter Group 2
A — Bas	Clo — Deb
Bat — Bom	Dec — Dov
Bon — Ceb	Dow — Em
Cec — Cli	En — Fic

Letter Group 3	Letter Group 4
Fid — Gaf	Id — Jis
Gag — Heg	Jit — Kol
Heh—Hum	Kom — Lam
Hun—Ic	Lan — Mej

Letter Group 5
Mek — Nar
Nas — Nub
Nuc — O
P — Pob

3. Print each of the following book entries on a different white card as shown here.

F Ale	Alexander, Anne
	   Connie; drawings by Gail Owens.
	   Atheneum 1976
	   179 p illus

F Blu	Blume, Judy
	   Blubber; Bradbury 1974
	   153p

F Bra	Branscum, Robbie
	   Johnny May; drawings by Charles
	   Robinson. Doubleday 1975
	   135 p illus

F Cle	Cleaver, Vera and Bill
	   Where the Lillies Bloom; drawings
	   by Jim Spanfeller. Lippincott 1969
	   174p illus

F
Cre
	Cresswell, Helen
	    Absolute Zero; Macmillan 1978
	    174p

F
Dix
	Dixon, Paige
	    Promises to Keep; Atheneum 1974
	    165p

F
Dun
	Duncombe, Frances
	    Summer of the Burning; illustrated
	    by Richard Cuffari. Putnam 1976
	    176p illus

F
Enr
	Enright, Elizabeth
	    Thimble Summer; illustrated by
	    Elizabeth Enright. Holt 1966
	    124p illus

F
Fox
	Fox, Paula
	    The Slave Dancer; drawings by Eros
	    Keith. Bradbury 1973
	    176p illus

F
Gre
	Greene, Bette
	    Summer of My German Soldier; Dial
	    1973
	    230p

F
Hic
	Hickman, Janet
	    Zoar Blue; Macmillan 1978
	    137p

F
Hun
	Hunt, Irene
	    William; Scribner's 1977
	    188p

F
Irw
	Irwin, Ann
	    One Bite at a Time; illustrated by
	    Nena Allen. Watts 1973
	    116 p illus

Library Skills Games

F
Jon
	Jones, Adrienne
	    So, Nothing Is Forever; drawings by
	    Richard Cuffari. Houghton Mifflin
	    1974
	    252p illus

F
Kon
	Konigsburg, E.L.
	    About the B'nai Bagels; illustrated
	    by E.L. Konigsburg. Atheneum 1971
	    172p illus

F
Low
	Lowry, Lois
	    A Summer to Die; drawings by Jenni
	    Oliver. Houghton Mifflin 1977
	    154p illus

F
Mil
	Miles, Betty
	    All It Takes Is Practice; Knopf
	    1976
	    101p

F
Ney
	Ney, John
	    Ox Goes North; Harper 1973
	    274p

F
Ode
	O'Dell, Scott
	    Zia; Houghton Mifflin 1976
	    179p

F
Pec
	Peck, Robert Newton
	    Soup for President; drawings by Ted
	    Lewin. Knopf 1978
	    107p illus

Library Skills Games

Game Play:

This game is for two to five players.

1. Each player chooses a brown gameboard. The white cards are placed in a stack face down in the center of the playing area.
2. The first player takes the top card and reads it. She looks over her gameboard to see if it will fit in one of her catalog drawers. If she finds one, she places the card in the slit above that drawer. If the player does not find an appropriate drawer, she discards the card, placing it face up next to the original card stack.
3. The next player continues the game in the same way. The first one to fill all slots in his gameboard is the winner. If the players use all of the cards in the original stack and there is still no winner, the cards not on the gameboards are turned over and play continues.

Library Skills Games

TRUCKIN' DOWN HIGHWAY 199

Skill Reinforced:

card catalog usage

Materials Needed:

1 sheet of 12" × 16" yellow posterboard
4 pieces of 3" × 2" posterboard each of a different color
30 pieces of 3" × 5" white posterboard
scissors
felt-tipped pen

Construction Directions:

1. Mark the yellow posterboard piece using an enlargement of the gameboard pattern shown here.

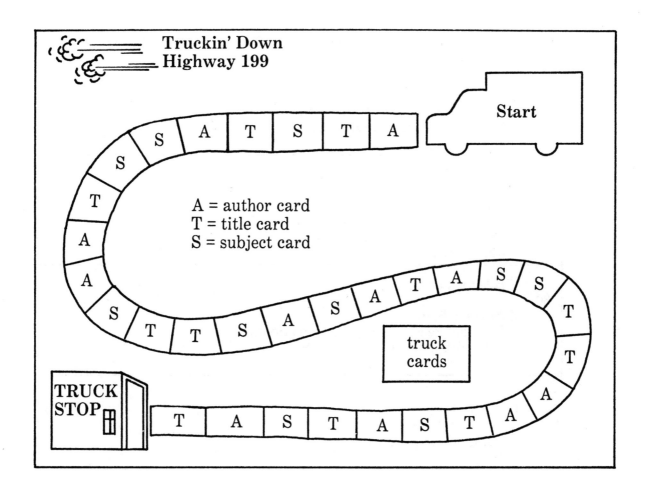

2. Cut the 3" × 2" posterboard pieces using the following truck pattern.

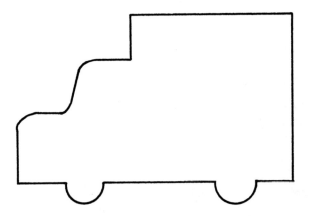

3. Print each of the following entries on a piece of white posterboard.

530
Z
	Zubrowski, Bernie
	    Ball-Point Pens; drawings by Linda Bourke.
	    Little, Brown and Company 1979
	    64p illus

530
Z
	PHYSICS—EXPERIMENTS
	
	Zubrowski, Bernie
	    Ball-Point Pens; drawings by Linda Bourke.
	    Little, Brown and Company 1979
	    64p illus

530
Z
	Ball-Point Pens
	
	Zubrowski, Bernie
	    Ball-Point Pens; drawings by Linda Bourke.
	    Little, Brown and Company 1979
	    64p illus

629
D
	Dwiggins, Don
	    Riders of the Winds;
	    Hawthorn Books 1973
	    180p illus

Library Skills Games

629
D
	BALLOONING
	
	Dwiggins, Don
	    Riders of the Winds;
	    Hawthorn Books 1973
	    180p illus

629
D
	Riders of the Winds
	
	Dwiggins, Don
	    Riders of the Winds;
	    Hawthorn Books 1973
	    180p illus

332
H
	Hintz, Sandy and Martin
	    We Can't Afford It; pictures by Brent Jones
	    Childrens Press 1977
	    30p illus

332
H
	SAVING AND THRIFT
	
	Hintz, Sandy and Martin
	    We Can't Afford It; pictures by Brent Jones
	    Childrens Press 1977
	    30p illus

332
H
	We Can't Afford It
	
	Hintz, Sandy and Martin
	    We Can't Afford It; pictures by Brent Jones
	    Childrens Press 1977
	    30p illus

523
G
	Gallant, Roy A.
	    Exploring Mars; illustrated by Lowell Hew
	    Doubleday 1968
	    61p illus

523
G
	MARS
	
	Gallant, Roy A.
	    Exploring Mars; illustrated by Lowell Hew
	    Doubleday 1968
	    61p illus

523
G
	Exploring Mars
	
	Gallant, Roy A.
	    Exploring Mars; illustrated by Lowell Hew
	    Doubleday 1968
	    61p illus

551
T
	Tannehill, Ivan Ray
	    All About the Weather; pictures by Rene Martin
	    Random House 1953
	    148p illus

551
T
	WEATHER
	
	Tannehill, Ivan Ray
	    All About the Weather; pictures by Rene Martin
	    Random House 1953
	    148p illus

551
T
	All About the Weather
	
	Tannehill, Ivan Ray
	    All About the Weather; pictures by Rene Martin
	    Random House 1953
	    148p illus

398
M
	Manning-Sanders, Ruth
	    A Book of Dragons; drawings by Robin Jacques
	    E.P. Dutton 1965
	    128p illus

398
M
	DRAGONS
	
	Manning-Sanders, Ruth
	    A Book of Dragons; drawings by Robin Jacques
	    E.P. Dutton 1965
	    128p illus

398
M
	A Book of Dragons
	
	Manning-Sanders, Ruth
	    A Book of Dragons; drawings by Robin Jacques
	    E.P. Dutton 1965
	    128p illus

Library Skills Games

523
A Asimov, Isaac
  What Makes the Sun Shine?; drawings by Marc Brown
  Little, Brown and Company 1971
  57p illus

SUN
523
A Asimov, Isaac
  What Makes the Sun Shine?; drawings by Marc Brown
  Little, Brown and Company 1971
  57p illus

What Makes the Sun Shine?
523
A Asimov, Isaac
  What Makes the Sun Shine?; drawings by Marc Brown
  Little, Brown and Company 1971
  57p illus

534
S Scott, John M.
  What Is Sound?; illustrated by Lawrence DiFiori
  Parents Magazine Press 1973
  64p illus

SOUND
534
S Scott, John M.
  What Is Sound?; illustrated by Lawrence DiFiori
  Parents Magazine Press 1973
  64p illus

What Is Sound?
534
S Scott, John M.
  What Is Sound?; illustrated by Lawrence DiFiori
  Parents Magazine Press 1973
  64p illus

325
D Dolan, Jr., Edward F.
  A Lion in the Sun
  Parents Magazine Press 1973
  280p

325
D
	GREAT BRITAIN
	
	Dolan, Jr., Edward F.
	   A Lion in the Sun
	   Parents Magazine Press 1973
	   280p

325
D
	A Lion in the Sun
	
	Dolan, Jr., Edward F.
	   A Lion in the Sun
	   Parents Magazine Press 1973
	   280p

639
O
	Ostermoller, Wolfgang
	   Aquarium Science
	   Harper & Row 1968
	   96p

639
O
	AQUARIUMS
	
	Ostermoller, Wolfgang
	   Aquarium Science
	   Harper & Row 1968
	   96p

639
O
	Aquarium Science
	
	Ostermoller, Wolfgang
	   Aquarium Science
	   Harper & Row 1968
	   96p

Library Skills Games

Game Play:

This game is for two to four players.

1. Each player chooses a truck marker and places it on **Start**. The word cards are placed face down in a stack on the gameboard.
2. The first player takes the top card and reads the information. Then he identifies it as an author, title, or subject card. If he is correct he moves his marker along the highway to the first space that contains the appropriate letter for the card he holds. If he is incorrect, he does not move his marker. The used card is placed on the bottom of the stack.
3. The next player continues the game in the same way. The first one to reach the end of the highway is the winner.

> **SUGGESTION:** You might include two or three cards that say "Flat Tire" or "Out of Gas," etc. If a player draws one of these, she loses a turn.

Library Skills Games

IN THIS BOOK?

Skill Reinforced:

index usage

Materials Needed:

3 sheets 9" × 7" blue posterboard
17 sheets 2" × 6" red posterboard
scissors
felt-tipped pen

Construction Directions:

1. Cut and mark the blue posterboard pieces using an enlargement of the book pattern shown here.

Library Skills Games

2. Print each of the following index groups on a separate book pattern.

Index Group I:

    Africa, 11, 12
       animals of, 72
       people of, 127
    Altitudes, 13-14
    Amphibia, 70
    Andes Mountains, 2
    Animals: desert adaptation of, 10
                domestic, 15
                mammals, 75
                tracks of, 104
                water requirements of, 83
    Antelopes, 72, 75
    Arabian Desert, 11
       plants of, 123
    Arabs, 126
       agriculture of, 29
       oil, 169
    Aridity: adaptation to, 53-54

Index Group II:

    Age of mountains, calculation of, 38
    Alaska, 12
    Aleutian Islands, 57
    Alps, 9
       age of, 17
       avalanches in, 28-31
       climbing peaks of, 158
       examples of folded mountains, 17
       farming in, 20-21
    Animals: on mountainsides, 13
                migration of, 109
                winter coats of, 109
    Appalachians, 37, 39
    Arctic Ocean, 31
    Asia: famous mountains of, 179
       mountain gaps in, 136
    Australia, 12
       famous mountains of, 109

Index Group III:

    Eagle, 111, 112
    Earth: gravitational pull of, 36
             layers of, 34
             surface of, 12
             temperatures inside, 34

Earth core, 34, 35, 36
Earth crust, 34
   changes in, 9-10
Earthquakes: defined, 34
                San Francisco, 36
                undersea, 61
Ecuador, 57, 82
Erosion, 10, 38
   effects of, 43
   glacial, 27
   importance of, for life, 12
   kinds of, 13
Europe:
   ice ages in, 14-15
   mountain belts of, 12
Everest, Mount, 11
   discovery of, 162-163

3. Cut and mark the red posterboard pieces using the book mark pattern shown here.

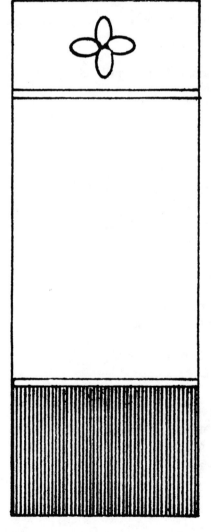

Library Skills Games

    4. Print each of the following on a different book mark.

        Miss a turn.
        Take an extra turn.
        Plants that grow on the Arabian Desert
        Information about the Andes Mountain Range
        Tracks that animals leave
        Food grown by Arabs
        How people have adapted to arid conditions
        How to tell the age of a mountain
        The location of the Aleutian Islands
        Facts about folded mountains
        What animals live on mountainsides
        Information about the Appalachian mountains
        The heat at the earth's core
        Who discovered Mount Everest
        Information about the ice ages in Europe
        How glaciers affect erosion
        The San Francisco earthquakes

Game Play:

This game is for two or three players.

1. Each player chooses a book gameboard. The bookmarks are placed in a stack, face down, in the center of the playing area.
2. The first player takes the top bookmark and reads the information. She then looks over her book gameboard to see if she could find the information in her index. If she can, she keeps the bookmark. If not, she places it, face down, on the bottom of the stack.
3. The next player continues the game in the same way.
4. The first player to collect five bookmarks is the winner.

DOWN PERISCOPE

Skill Reinforced:

encyclopedia usage

Materials Needed:

1 sheet 12" × 16" blue posterboard
2 sheets 2" × 3½" gray posterboard
25 sheets 2" × 3" white posterboard
scissors
felt-tipped pen

Construction Directions:

1. Mark the blue posterboard piece using an enlargement of the gameboard pattern shown here.

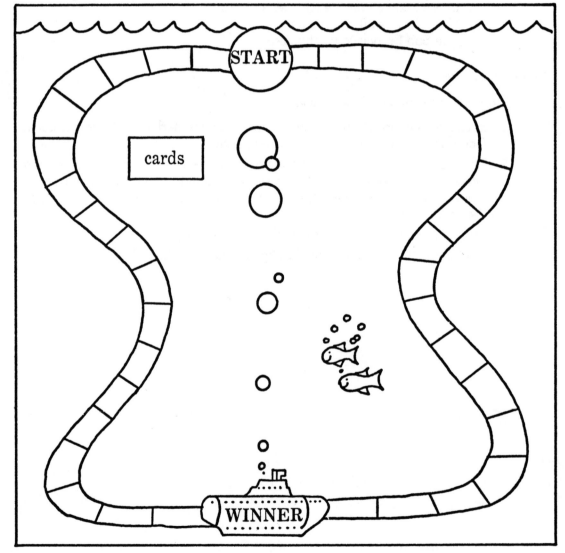

Library Skills Games

2. Cut and mark the gray posterboard pieces using the submarine pattern shown here.

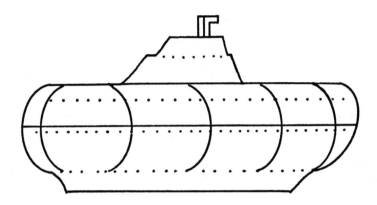

3. Print each of the following on a separate white card.

    Floor plan of your school building
    Location of your local hospitals
    Telephone numbers of congressmen
    Beginner recipes for cooking
    The Greyhound bus schedule
    Strong Currents! Go back one space.
    Engine Trouble! Go back one space.
    Parts of flowers
    How the eye works
    The causes of the ocean's tides
    Kinds of forests in our world
    The active volcanoes in our world
    A brief biography of George Washington
    How the Supreme Court functions
    Facts about comets
    Information about tropical fish
    Kinds of domestic cats
    Information about Great Britain
    A map of Argentina
    Information about New York City
    How paper is made
    The past presidents of the United States
    How motion pictures work
    Information about fine art
    The government system of Canada

Game Play:

This game is for two players.

1. Each player chooses a submarine and places it on the start bubble. The cards are placed face down in a stack on the gameboard.
2. The first player takes the top card and reads it. If the information can be found in an encyclopedia, she moves her submarine one space along the left-hand path to the WINNER spot. If not, she simply places the card on the bottom of the stack.

    NOTE: There are two cards which force the player to move his submarine "back" one space.

3. The next player continues the game in the same way moving his submarine along the right-hand path. The first player to reach the WINNER spot on the gameboard is the winner.

Library Skills Games

CHAMP

Skill Reinforced:

guide word usage

Materials Needed:

6 sheets 9" × 9" red posterboard
6 circles 8" diameter white posterboard
6 paper fasteners
15 sheets 3" × 6" yellow posterboard
scissors
felt-tipped pen

Construction Directions:

1. Cut the sheets of red posterboard and attach the white circles as shown here.

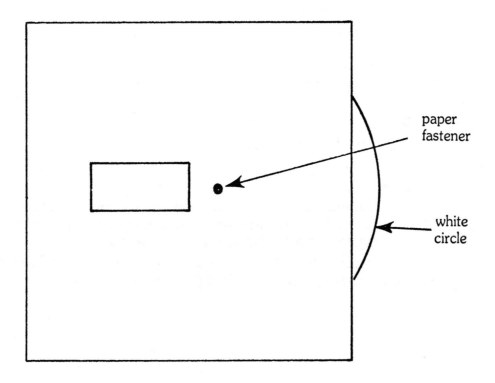

Library Skills Games

2. In the window cutout, write the following words on the white circles, turning them for each new entry.

baby	backward
bait	batter
balk	beach
balm	beam
bang	beat
bare	bee
barrier	begun
basement	

3. Copy each of the following pairs of guide words on a different yellow card.

   babble — bachelor
   background — badger
   bail — balance
   bald — ball
   balloon — band
   bandage — bank
   baptize — bark
   baron — barter
   base — basket
   bath — bay
   bayou — beak
   bead — bear
   beard — beauty
   bed — beetle
   beggar — believe

Game Play:

This game is for three to six players.

1. One player is chosen as caller and scorekeeper. Each player receives a red gameboard.
2. The caller holds up a yellow card so all players can see it at the same time. These are guide words. Each player turns the circle on his gameboard until he finds a word that will fit between these guide words.
3. The first player to find it receives a "C." Play continues until one player has spelled the word "CHAMP." This player is the winner.

Library Skills Games

CECIL'S LOTTO GAME

Skill Reinforced:

Dewey decimal classification

Materials Needed:

5 sheets 7" × 9" white posterboard
30 circles of red posterboard with 2" diameters
30 gummed green circles with 2" diameters
felt-tipped pen

Construction Directions:

1. Copy "Cecil" on each of the large sheets of posterboard and place the gummed circles around him as shown in the illustration.

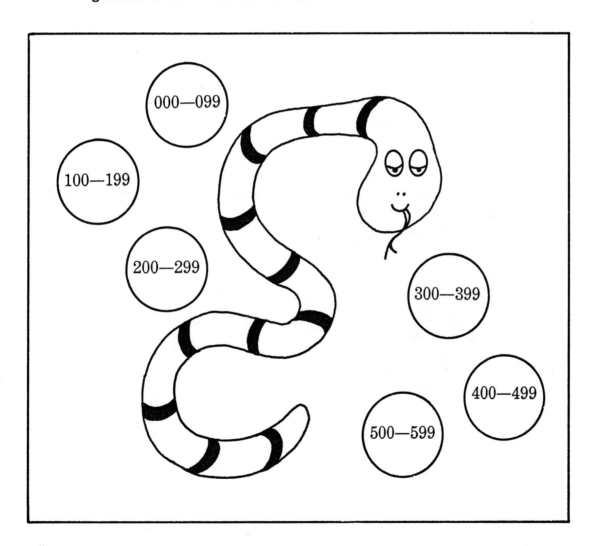

271

2. Mark the following Dewey decimal numerals on the gummed circles as shown in the illustration.

   Gameboard 1:
   - 000–099
   - 100–199
   - 200–299
   - 300–399
   - 400–499
   - 500–599

   Gameboard 2:
   - 200–299
   - 300–399
   - 400–499
   - 500–599
   - 600–699
   - 700–799

   Gameboard 3:
   - 400–499
   - 500–599
   - 600–699
   - 700–799
   - 800–899
   - 900–999

   Gameboard 4:
   - 000–099
   - 200–299
   - 400–499
   - 600–699
   - 700–799
   - 800–899

   Gameboard 5:
   - 100–199
   - 300–399
   - 500–599
   - 600–699
   - 800–899
   - 900–999

3. Print each one of the following Dewey decimal classifications on three of the red posterboard circles.

   - Social Sciences
   - Religion
   - Pure Science
   - Literature
   - Language
   - The Arts
   - Philosophy
   - History
   - General Works
   - Technology

Library Skills Games

Game Play:

This game is for two to five players.

1. Each player takes a gameboard. The circles are placed in a stack face down in front of the players.
2. The first player picks a circle. If she can match it with one of the Dewey decimal numerals on her card, she keeps the circle and places it on top of the numerals. If not, she puts the circle back on the bottom of the stack and the next player takes her turn.
3. The first player to fill his card is the winner.

Library Skills Games

WHICH CATEGORY?

Skill Reinforced:

Dewey decimal classification

Materials Needed:

10 sheets 6" × 6" yellow posterboard
10 sheets 2" × 6" white posterboard
scissors
felt-tipped pen

Construction Directions:

1. Cut and mark the yellow pieces of posterboard as shown in the illustration.

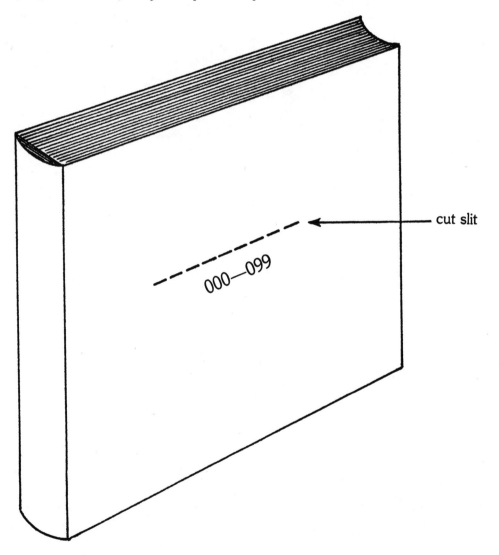

Library Skills Games

2. Print each of the following Dewey decimal classifications on a different book as shown in the illustration. Print each of the corresponding numerals in parentheses on the backs of the books.

   (1) 000-099 (6) 500-599
   (2) 100-199 (7) 600-699
   (3) 200-299 (8) 700-799
   (4) 300-399 (9) 800-899
   (5) 400-499 (10) 900-999

3. Mark the white posterboard pieces as shown here.

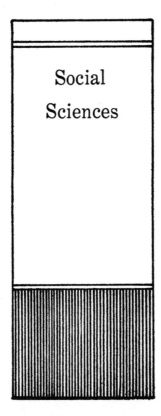

4. Print each of the following categories on a different bookmark as shown in the illustration. Print the corresponding numeral on the back of each of the bookmarks.

   (1) General Works (6) Pure Science
   (2) Philosophy   (7) Technology
   (3) Religion   (8) The Arts
   (4) Social Sciences (9) Literature
   (5) Language   (10) History

Game Play:

This game may be played by one player.

1. Put the books in one pile and the bookmarks in another.
2. Take the top book and look at the numerals. You are to find the correct bookmark for this book according to the Dewey decimal classification. When you think you have found it, place the bookmark in the slot in the book and continue to do the same with the rest of the bookmarks.
3. When you are finished, turn over the game pieces. If the numerals on the backs of each pair of cards are the same, you are correct.

Skills Index

Alphabetization:

    Answer the Telephone, 237
    Be a Sport!, 176
    Candy Factory, 107
    Dave's Birthday, 159
    Follow the Rainbow, 116
    Grand Prix, 216
    Great Animals of the Past, 187
    High-Rise Apartments!, 183
    Key Ring, 207
    Presidents Puzzle, 179
    Help Robbie Rabbit, 110
    Shipshape, 155
    Stairway to the Moon, 158
    Tree Mania!, 182
    A Trip to Planet Gleet!, 119
    Through the Night Sky, 218
    A Whale of a Good Time, 208

Atlas Usage:

    Deep in the Ocean, 190
    Hang It!, 245
    The High Jump, 193
    See How High You Can Fly the Kite, 138

Card Catalog Usage:

    Climb the Mountain, 220
    Crazy Cards, 247
    Find the Drawer, 250
    It's Raining, 123
    Oh Gosh!, 177
    Spin Out, 226
    Suppose You Knew ..., 178
    Truckin' Down Highway 199, 255
    Which Drawer?, 164

Dewey Decimal Classification:

    An Artist, 174
    Be an Artist!, 83
    Blooming Books, 72
    Cecil's Lotto Game, 271
    Follow the Flock!, 197
    Food for Thought, 66
    In Chicago!, 199
    The Mystery at Skull Mountain, 198
    Sailing, 132
    Unlock These Doors to Good Reading!, 89
    Very Berry, 175
    Which Category?, 274
    Who Let in the Dog?, 196

Dictionary Skills:

    A "Monsterous" Vocabulary, 146
    Pick a Balloon, 224
    Symbols of America, 172

Encyclopedia Usage:

    The Big "E", 230
    Blast Off!, 215
    Can You Picture This?, 141
    Down Periscope, 266
    Help for Jack!, 194
    The Surprise!, 186
    A Visit to Their Grandparents, 184
    Walk Through the Forest, 191

Fiction from Nonfiction:

    Crossing Death Valley, 171
    Oh No!, 170
    Robin's Roost, 126

Skills Index

General Library Knowledge:

    Bee in the Know, 42
    Word Search Puzzle, 200

Guide Word Usage:

    Champ, 269
    Dogs … Dogs … Dogs!, 180
    Guide Word Puzzle, 181
    My Favorite!, 169
    Rockets Away!, 232
    Sad Sack, 235
    Score!, 129
    Ski Jumping, 166
    Take a Train Ride, 163

Index Usage:

    Apples, Oranges, and Lemons, 212
    The Balloon That Got Away!, 160
    How Do You Know?, 161
    In This Book?, 262
    Index Information, 188
    Let's Take a Trip!, 165
    Look It Up!, 189
    Surfing!, 135

Knowledge of Books and Authors:

    Basket of the Best, 39
    Be a Book Promoter, 45
    Book Jacket Puzzles, 39
    Book Lists for Children, 18
    Book Mobiles, 10

Knowledge of Books and Authors: (con'td)

    Books About Our People!, 102
    Kick Up Your Heels … and Write a Letter to an Author!, 77
    Nobel Prize for Literature, 100
    A Peach of a Good Book, 40
    Vote for Your Favorite "Little House" Book!, 91
    Who Murdered Lady Quackle?, 94
    Write to Your Favorite Author, 41

Location of Fiction Books on Shelves:

    Arrange the Books, 162
    Feed The Elephants!, 113
    Follow the Rainbow, 168
    Shelve 'Em!, 242
    Traveling by Rail, 210
    What Country Are We In?, 167
    Where's the Book?, 148
    Who Shelved This?, 243

Table of Contents Usage:

    Buzz Off!, 185
    Colorful Contents, 192
    It's Ancient History, 195
    Match to Win!, 239
    Quacker Questions, 143
    Something's Fishy, 222
    Table "Twirl" of Contents, 228
    A Table of What?, 157
    What a Score!, 173